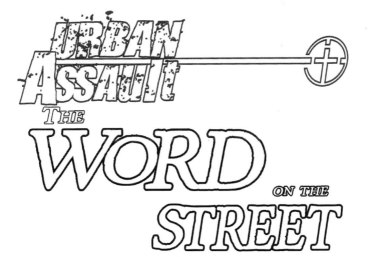

URBAN ASSAULT
THE WORD ON THE STREET

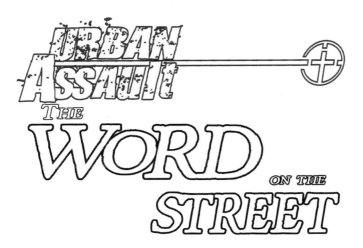

URBAN ASSAULT
THE WORD ON THE STREET

eheapress•San Pablo•California

Urban Assault: The Word on the Street

JDMorgan

Richard Blake: editor

Copyright © 2013 by James D. Morgan
ISBN: 978-0-9898577-0-3

Published by eheapress, a division of Eleventh Hour
Evangelistic Association 106 San Pablo Towne Center, San
Pablo, California 94806
Printed in the United States of America.

Cover artwork: Creative by Design
Cover photography: Michael Chissell

DEDICATION

In memory of:

Terrie Bullock-Morgan, Mary Morgan-Reed, Leatha Hendricks, Lola Latchison, Georgia Haynes, Bishop Columbus Williams and Bishop W. Wesley Sanders

TABLE OF CONTENTS

ACKNOWLEDGEMENTS

Evangelists Ron Haynes and Pastor A. J. Latchison who "baptized" me into the ministry of evangelism through street crusades and prison outreach more than thirty years ago.

Dick Blake for your sharp editorial pen and more-than-frequent consultations.

Rev. Elreta Dodds, Eld. Samson Dyson, Don Buchholz, Rochelle Monk, Pastor Jon Drury and the Castro Valley Christian Writer's Group for your encouragement and objective critiques.

My Pastor; Bishop J. W. Macklin for your unwavering support and for setting the high standard for excellence in ministry.

Vaughn, Damita, Brandon, David, Erinn and James for believing in me (I love you)

The Urban Apologetic

The term apologetics is derived from the Greek word apologia, which was used to mean to defend or to vindicate. In ancient courts of law, when a plaintiff brought an accusation against someone, that person was allotted time for a rebuttal or defense in response to the charge. In its early years, Christianity came under intense scrutiny and attack from philosophers and religious sects as Jesus was introduced as the Son of God and the Savior of an increasingly pagan world. As a result, it became necessary for those who were well versed in the Faith to establish a relevant response based in historic fact and sound reasoning. Among the early apologists were Justin Martyr, Irenaeus of Lyons, Augustine of Hippo, and Clement of Alexandria. I would add to that list those I consider to be the great apologists of our era; C.S. Lewis, Josh McDowell and Dr. Ravi Zacharias.

When I consider the unique way of life in the inner-city ghetto, I am convinced that a new standard of defending the faith is called for—the Urban Apologetic. If there is no such term as urban apologetics, perhaps there should be, because there is a marked difference between the urban and suburban cultures. There are some things that are peculiar to the urban experience that differentiate it from the more socially acceptable "norm" of the suburbs. Racism, poverty, corrupt leaders, dysfunctional or non-existent families, under-funded schools and over-funded prisons have created an urban jungle where people have become hardened to a lifestyle of drug dealing and exploiting others as the most viable means of generating income. Here, the incarceration of so many marginalized citizens has given birth to a culture where kindness is equated with weakness and where violence has become a means of gaining power and respect.

Themes of social justice, racial injustice, unemployment and crime all weigh heavily in the urban subconscious and, by definition, should be included in the lexicon of urban apologetics. These issues have become part of the fabric of the urban experience, and should be considered in any discussion of a relevant faith. Moreover, it is concern over these matters that may provide a credible means for sharing the Faith.

One of my personal heroes, Dr. John Perkins founded a national organization based on the principle of sharing the Faith by ministering to what he calls the felt needs of those persons he wanted to reach with the Gospel. In meeting those felt needs, or the needs that seemed most pressing in the minds of the people he ministered to, Dr. Perkins instituted the Christian Community Development Association, providing housing assistance, educational facilities, and co-op stores. As a direct result of this ministry, souls have made decisions to receive salvation (some even from the volunteers who helped) through a relevant Christian witness where the faith is lived out in practical ministry.

And relevance is a key factor in relating the Gospel, particularly when it comes to those who would challenge the validity of a faith that doesn't seem connected to the urban reality. And in many ways, the church is disconnected from the urban reality, particularly in the minds of those who live it.

I attended a community forum sponsored by a Faith-based non-profit organization. The focus of the meeting was on developing programs to help at risk youth. During the lunch break, I overheard a comment from one of the attendees, and I paraphrase; I don't go to church because the church is not doing anything in the community.

In urban centers across America, Christian churches occupy almost every corner; many, in neighborhoods where violent crime, abject poverty and substance abuse have become accepted facts of life. Yet, many pastors believe that a major short coming of the urban church is the lack of evangelism. And in the absence of a credible witness in the community, attitudes toward the church have changed and so have attitudes toward the relevancy of its message.

In order to capture (or re-capture) the relevance of the Gospel message to the inner city, we must move out of the confines of our sanctuaries—not just in preaching, singing and handing out tracts—but in touching the lives of those that God has charged us to "bring in hither". And that is the purpose of this work; to draw attention to the peculiar needs of the urban community, to make the case for the urgent need to reach our streets with the Gospel, and to Empower, Equip and Engage the Body of Christ for ministry to the 'hood.

.

PART

1

THE CALL

CHAPTER ONE

MAKING THE CASE FOR URBAN EVANGELISM

*"But if the watchman see the sword come, and blow not the
trumpet, and the people be not warned; if the sword come,
and take any person from among them, he is taken away in
his iniquity; but his blood will I require at the watchman's
hand."*

(Ezekiel 33:6)

"THE RIVER OF BLOOD THAT WASHES THE STREETS OF OUR
NATION... FLOWS MOSTLY FROM THE BODIES OF OUR BLACK
CHILDREN... WHY ARE WE MUTE? WHERE ARE OUR LEADERS;
OUR LEGISLATORS? WHERE IS THE CHURCH?"

HARRY BELAFONTE

WHERE IS THE CHURCH?

I watched Harry Belafonte—living legend and personal hero—as he accepted the Lifetime Achievement Award during the 2013 NAACP Image Awards. It wasn't the eloquence, but the content of his acceptance speech that held me captive to my television. His challenge and his charge to the church burned in my mind long after the screen had gone dark and his speech had ended. I was challenged at the place of my faith and at the point of my commitment—not just as an individual, but as one who professes to be a part of the very church he challenged. The question would not let me rest that night.

Where is the church?

I am aware that there are numerous churches and faith-based organizations that have committed themselves to community and civic duty, but for the most part the evangelistic voice of the church—the one true calling of the church that can actually bring about the change we so desperately need—has all but been silenced.

To be sure, we've rallied, marched and protested; but divisions over race and denomination and a refocus of ministry on success and self-affirmation have rendered the voice of evangelism virtually silent.

I'm not sure if it was the question that disturbed me, or the fact that it was asked.

The perception that the church was somehow derelict in its duty to reach out to the inner city; the idea that we are missing in action while our cities suffer; the thought that the church is unconcerned about the plight of our communities (whether real or imagined) should disturb us at the core of our being.

And if it is true that we are guilty of being silent, then the prophetic words of Ezekiel should disturb us even moreso. Because we are charged before God to be the watchmen of the city, to warn the people against the impending disaster and to call our communities to a right relationship with God, He holds *us* accountable for the "river of blood" that literally washes our streets.

Possibly without realizing it we have turned our focus inward, concentrating our energies on building bigger churches. In our effort to draw nearer to God, perhaps we have withdrawn ourselves from the communities that need us. Maybe in the interest of *having* church, we have forgotten how to *be* the church. And so Mr. Belafonte's question confronts us... challenges us... charges us.

Where is the church?

Today, I received a humorous e-mail from a friend. It was one of those—why don't they?—list of silly, but sometimes relevant questions. Among the questions, this one caught my attention; "Why doesn't Mapquest provide directions around the ghetto?"

Though my friend thought his note was light and humorous, I mulled over the thought—and the sentiment behind it. And that sentiment spoke volumes to me concerning our (not so) unspoken desire to avoid the unpleasantness of touching and being touched by the ghetto... or the people who live there.

Too many of our churches have removed themselves from the problem, and taken our resources (and our God) with us. So, I put the question to the Lord; "Don't you care about what's happening to our people?"

The answer came as God began to reveal His heart for the ghetto and He directed me to the familiar story of the woman at the well recorded in the gospel of St. John. This time, however, He directed my attention—not to the woman—but to the city she came from, and to the many similarities between ancient Samaria and today's inner-city.

JESUS IN THE 'HOOD

"And He must needs go through Samaria "
St. John 4:4

In the gospel of St. John, the Bible records this period of Jesus' ministry as he introduces himself as the Messiah. In this passage, we find the Lord leaving Judea on his way to Galilee, the writer notes; " ...he must needs go through Samaria" or in the NKJV ; "He needed to go through Samaria." This passage of Scripture captures my interest because it reveals God's concern for what we would think of as the "bad" part of town. And through Jesus' example, he sets the standard for the church to transcend racial and socioeconomic barriers to reach those souls in need of a savior.

Another reason I find this passage interesting is that the writer would find it necessary to make the statement; "he needed to go through Samaria" since Samaria was the province situated directly between Judea and Galilee and any travel from one place to the other would leave little choice except a trip through Samaria.

The phrase; "must needs" suggest that it was by force of circumstance or needful that Jesus go through Samaria. Needful for what or for whom? Perhaps it was for the sake of expediency, in the interest of saving time, or for the sake of provisions; food, rest, lodging; or maybe Jesus needed to go through Samaria, not for his own sake, but for the sake of the Samaritans.

Unique, not only for its location, but for its history and the history of its people, Samaria was a division of the Canaan-land that had been promised by God to the descendants of Abraham, Isaac and Jacob and allotted to the tribes of Ephraim and Manasseh. According to Hosea 7:1 and 8:5-7 this was a fertile land that produced much of the wealth in the region.

The Capital city of Samaria was founded by Omri, sixth king of Israel, in 880 BC, and became a center of commerce and culture until its overthrow by the Assyrians in 722 BC.

Samaria held a sacred place in the heart of the Jews. In Genesis 33:18-19, the Bible records that this was the parcel of land that had been purchased by Jacob and the place where he built an altar to honor God which he called El-elohe-Israel which translates "Mighty One; God of Israel". In Mt. Ebal of Samaria, was the site where Joshua renewed the Covenant between God and Israel. This was the place where the tribes of Israel buried the bones of their patriarch, Joseph. And here in Samaria, King Sargon of Assyria forcefully took the descendants of Abraham, Isaac and Jacob into captivity and replaced them with the pagan peoples of Babylon, Cuthah, Ava, Hamath and Separvaim.

Stripped from their countries of origin, these nations began to inter-marry across their own racial and cultural boundaries as well as with the remnant of Hebrews who had been deemed to be less educated, less skillful and less worthy by the Assyrians, and who for that reason, had been left to live in Samaria. As a result, this new race of Samaritans (as they came to be called) was of a mixed ethnicity; a blended people whose ties to any cultural heritage or national identity had been erased over time.

Now, rather than identifying themselves by the land of their origin, they only knew themselves as Samaritan, having no distinct identity apart from the one that had been given to them by the government that placed them there.

Through no fault of their own, the Samaritans bore the iniquity of being an impure race (at least by Jewish standards) occupying a country they hadn't paid for either in labor or in blood, placed there by an insensitive government. Held to account for a relocation program that they had no voice in creating, the Samaritans became as much the victims of the process as the landowners they displaced.

Moreover, because the Samaritans continued to worship the pagan idols of their former cultures in the land that the Hebrews had consecrated to God, God cursed the land. And where it had once been a center of culture and commerce it had become a troublesome and dangerous place... a cursed place. And almost as if to add insult to injury, the king of Assyria (in an attempt to turn back the wrath of God) required the Jewish priests to teach the Samaritans the ways of the God of Abraham.

Because of this, the Samaritans came to embrace the same hope of redemption and waited for the same promise of the Messiah as did the Jew. So, not only were Samaritans seen as unwelcome trespassers in the Promised Land, but now they had the audacity to lay claim to the Jews inheritance of faith. And for these *unpardonable sins* the Jews despised the Samaritans, or at the least, tolerated them. And for this cause, Jews would completely bypass the region of Samaria, choosing rather to take the route east along the Jordan River rather than risk any contact with Samaria or the Samaritans.

Understanding the history of Samaria and of its people and their relationship to the Jews, it becomes more significant that the writer would draw our attention to the *not so* obvious point:

He must needs go through Samaria

For a Rabbi, teacher or the leader of a sect, it would be political suicide to be seen in Samaria. For a descendant of the House of David, it would be a social disgrace to be associated with these racially and ceremonially impure people. But, for Jesus the Messiah, it was of a necessity that he go through Samaria. Being of Jewish descent, Jesus knew the troubled history of Samaria and of the strained relationship between the two races.

As a Jew, Jesus knew that Samaria was a place that had been abandoned by the upright and avoided by the righteous. As a Jew, Jesus could have chosen to follow the culturally accepted practice and travelled east around the Jordan, sparing himself (and his reputation) any contact with Samaria. But as the Messiah, Jesus saw Samaria as a place that needed to hear the Good News of the gospel. As the Messiah, Jesus didn't look on the fallen state of the city or the Samaritans. And as the Messiah, Jesus looked beyond all those things that the righteous would call unclean or ungodly and saw a people in need of salvation.

Today—just as the church did in Jesus' time— we have built super highways and overpasses that afford us the convenience of bypassing our Samaria. We can drive past the *bad part of town* without acknowledging the people in it, caring to know who they are or how they came to be there. We don't have to look at the faces of the broken, or into the eyes of the hopeless, or share, even briefly, the Samaritan experience. We have the luxury of bypassing the plight of our Samaria, and its Samaritans. But just as He did then, Jesus still sees *Samaria* as a place that needs to hear the Good News of the gospel. Jesus still looks beyond all those things that we would call unclean or ungodly and sees a people in need of salvation.

THE NEEDFUL NOW

"...Go out quickly into the streets and lanes of the city, and bring in hither the poor, and the maimed, and the halt, and the blind."

Luke14:21b

In the gospel of St. Luke, Jesus challenges his disciples to move out of the comfort of their close-knit company to go quickly into the streets of the city, to reach beyond the boundaries and the bonds of their own fellowship to embrace an unlikely group;

"The poor, and the maimed, and the halt, and the blind."

This was the heart of Jesus' ministry, those who were not only down-trodden, but who had been trodden down; the poor, the emotionally and psychologically broken, those with physical, educational and social limitations; those whose dreams had been abbreviated, and those who were either unable or unwilling to see. Not only were the disciples called to go out and interact with this hurting community, but to bring them into the fellowship of the believers. Jesus' charge to go out also came with a pressing call to do what had to be done in the now and with a sense of urgency.

" Go out quickly "

Quickly-speedily, rapidly, without delay.

Quickly- full-tilt, fast, hot-foot.

Quickly- immediately, instantaneously, now!

Looking at the definition of the word *quickly*, the apparent but unspoken message appears to be that time was of the essence, and the need to act was critical.

Maybe the need for urgency was because of the increasing crime in the area, or the number of children who were suffering in poverty. Maybe it was the breakdown of the family unit, or because the people had begun to destroy their own lives through substance abuse. Or maybe it was Jesus' unique ability to empathize with the needs of those who were hurting and without hope that prompted His call to act quickly. Whatever the motivation, Jesus was absolute in affirming that the need take the message of salvation to the street was crucial and immediate.

And today; as crime and poverty rates increase by the hour and the destabilization of the urban family has become an accepted fact of life, and as the drug culture has so entrenched itself in our urban centers, that same sense of urgency calls out to us from inner cities across America. And the need to take the message of salvation to the streets of the city is crucial and immediate.

THE AMERICAN URBAN CRISIS

In the streets and lanes of today's cities, self-destructive behavior, substance abuse and drug related violence have become the reality. The acquisition of drugs and deadly weapons has become as easy as a trip to the local Kwik-mart, and prison-based gangs are recruiting young children who have no ties to family, community or to the church. As a consequence, over 1,000 African American children are arrested every day. Of those arrests, 102 are for violent crimes and 119 are for drug violations. Every day 6,916 black students are suspended from a public school while 417 children simply drop out. [1]

The murder rate in the inner cities has reached such epidemic proportions that on any given day, three black children die as a direct result of gunfire. And the disproportionate arrest and incarceration of inner city youth has only served to create an environment where time in jail or juvenile hall has come to be seen as a rite of passage.

In 1968, Dr. Kenneth B. Clark predicted the dire future of America's urban centers with an almost prophetic accuracy. In the Report of the National Advisory Commission on Civil Disorders, Clark wrote;

> With the father absent and the mother working, many
> ghetto children spend the bulk of their time on the
> streets – the streets of a crime-ridden, violence-prone
> and poverty-stricken world... The culture of poverty that
> results from unemployment and family disorganization
> generates a system of ruthless, exploitative relationships
> within the ghetto. Prostitution, dope addiction, casual
> sexual affairs, and crime create an environmental jungle
> characterized by personal insecurity and tension.[2]

Clark went on to point out the inescapable reality
that if the   issues   of inferior housing, inferior
education and job discrimination were not seriously
and immediately addressed, people who are forced
to live in those conditions should not be expected to
show respect for the property of others or for the order
of the law.

At her own peril, America chose to ignore this
impending crisis. And as a penalty, today we face
the disintegration of the family, the disproportionate
arrests and convictions of a *criminalized** under-class,
and the creation of a violent inner city subculture.

Well over half of America's black children live without
fathers in the household, more than twice the rate of
Latino children and three times that of white children.
Of the black men between ages twenty-five and thirty-
four who have dropped out of high school, seventy-
five percent are in prison or on parole.[3] Of the African
American males from ages eighteen to thirty-four, at

least one third are under the authority of the criminal justice system; either in jail, on probation, or with a case pending trial.[4] And as the minority population shifts from predominantly African American to Latin American, the numbers in arrests and conviction are rapidly shifting as well.

Author Herbert J. Hoelter notes that, while African Americans comprise only thirteen percent of the national population and fourteen percent of its drug users, they make up seventy-five percent of those imprisoned for substance abuse, the cause for a majority of arrests.[5]

With the incarceration of so many African and Latin Americans, our inner cities have become a *prison-ized* culture where the entire community is shaped by the prison experience. As inmates are cycled in and out of the revolving prison doors, the harsh prison subculture has become the defining culture of the streets. In this pitiless environment, human compassion has come to be seen as a weakness, violent behavior has become a way to exert power and influence, and the exploitation of the weak has become an acceptable means of survival.

In addition to the corruptive impact of incarceration, the glorification of the hard-core "gangsta" lifestyle by the media has created such a destructive mind-set that youth have come to accept violent behavior as a normal part of ghetto life, and the cycle of violence, prison and poverty is perpetuated.

In the book *Envy of the World*, author Ellis Cose speaks to the heart of this issue:

> By running so many persons through jails and prisons each year, the violent ethos of the correctional facility has increasingly come to shape behavior on the streets and undermine respect for the law.

> Prison life permeates everything about the community and keeps it down. That's all young people have to look forward to... their role models are involved in gang and drug activity. To them, it's a normal process to transition from the streets to prison.[6]

As I began researching information for this chapter, I was offended by some of the more conservative writers who suggested that America's inner cities had become an amoral jungle. I took offense, or more truthfully, I became angry because the jungle reference has ties to old racial slurs that equated African Americans to savage natives with sub-human intelligence and tendencies toward animalistic behavior. But later, I was moved from anger to anguish, because as I began writing this segment, I read a news report of one of the most savage attacks I could have ever imagined.

In Cleveland, Ohio fifteen gang members literally kicked and beat a man to death, stripped the clothes from his body and urinated on his head in public view. The suspects charged with the murder were 19, 20 and 23 years old! More recently, international headlines reported the gang rape of a 16 year old student that took place at a high school prom, while onlookers videotaped the act for broadcast on the internet. But what troubles me more than the savage nature of these attacks, is the brutal and sadistic spirit behind them. A spirit that is becoming more pervasive as society becomes more de-sensitized to the cruelty of these crimes.

I know that these crimes do not reflect the moral makeup of the whole of the city, neither do they justify the blanket stigma; "jungle" as applied by some writers. But the fact that inner city children grow up in the constant awareness of death, that they learn at an early age to cope with the trauma of losing classmates and loved ones to random gunfire, or the fact that every child in the city is either related to or acquainted with someone who is or has been incarcerated should signal the fact that our inner cities are at a critical stage. And when you add the HIV/AIDS epidemic, the problem is multiplied exponentially.

According to a report from the Center for Disease Control and Prevention, although African Americans are only thirteen percent of the population, they make up forty-nine percent of the HIV/AIDS cases in the U.S.; sixty-five percent of infants born with the virus and sixty-one percent of those infected under the age of twenty-five. And as of 2010, one in twenty-two African Americans will be diagnosed with AIDS—in contrast to one in fifty-two Latin Americans and one in one hundred-seventy whites. [7]

Even with government studies and programs, and with warnings from executive think tanks from more than thirty years ago, America's inner cities are still in crisis. And at the center of this crisis... God has left His church.

THE AMERICAN URBAN WITNESS

Whether as converted warehouses, conventional worship centers, or humble storefronts, the Christian church occupies almost every corner of America's inner cities. And it appears that the more economically depressed the area, the greater the church presence. And yet, with the church as such a prominent part of inner city life; gang violence, substance abuse and teen prostitution still persist.

There are many inner city churches that provide missions-based services; food banks, rehabilitation centers and housing assistance, but these programs and initiatives only appear to address the physical and social need. A listing of African American religious organizations compiled by the Howard University School of Divinity illustrates the fact that most religious bodies; including major denominations, interfaith conventions and faith-based non-profits are more focused on leadership development, scholarship funding, and community development.[8] And while I find these areas of civic engagement extremely relevant to social change, I'm convinced that they lack the key element for the transformational change that is really needed... transformation of the individual.

As our churches seek to provide for the social needs of marginalized people, we have to consider that feeding, clothing and housing a person who has not been regenerated will only produce a well fed, well dressed but ultimately unchanged individual. I have been made aware, recently, of an evangelistic awakening that is taking place in the inner city faith community across the country (actually, more with individuals and individual ministries), but these efforts generally don't represent the central focus of the mainstream church. For too many churches in the inner cities, it appears that the central focus has become internal; faith building, fellowship and financial success.

In a survey taken by C. Eric Lincoln and Lawrence H. Mamiya, inner city pastors revealed an unsettling reality. Of the pastors interviewed, almost half believe that the leading problem facing the black church is the lack of evangelism in fulfilling its religious role. [9] It seems that the majority of inner city churches have become insular, or inwardly focused, with most ministry efforts directed toward their own needs; building expansions and improvements, fund raising for church related projects, with the membership occupied in activities that keep them tied to the physical church.

In the book *Introducing the Missional Church*, writers Alan J. Roxburgh and M. Scott Boren make this observation:

> "...[M]uch of the focus in the church has become about church survival or turning around churches for the sake of preserving the church as it is known." [10]

This internal ministry focus, in contrast to an external outreach driven focus, only serves to create a separation between the church and the people the church is called to serve.

THE SEPARATION OF CHURCH AND STATE

"Wherefore come ye out from among them, and be ye separate, saith the Lord.."

(2 Corinthians 6:14-17)

Our version of The Separation of Church and State seems to have taken this verse to mean that we are to keep ourselves apart and separate from the ungodly sinner and associate solely with other believers. While this call to separation may be based in the biblical precept of avoiding evil associations, in many cases our understanding of this call has also created a wall of division between the Christian and those we are called to reach. An example of this comes from an experience that was shared by a personal friend; a former drug lord who became addicted to the very poison he sold to others.

As I was conducting a seminar on outreach, I came to the passage of Scripture found in John 4:35; "Lift up your eyes and look on the fields" to illustrate the point that many of us in the Household of Faith don't want to look at the unlovely reality of the streets and those we are charged to reach. For many of us, I added, it is easier to avoid making eye contact by looking the other way. At that point in the presentation, my friend stood up, not content to raise his hand and wait to be recognized. As he spoke, his voice broke, his eyes filled with tears and he shared the story of how he had become tired of his lifestyle and wanted to be free from his addictions.

Being raised in the church, he knew that the only real help for him was through those who knew the Lord. The tears began to flow, as he told how he staggered out of the crack-house one morning to find a group of Christians making their way to the sanctuary for Sunday worship. But when they saw him, they crossed to the other side of the street to avoid any contact with him. So, while they may have arrived at the church safely and with their sanctity intact; they missed the opportunity to reach a soul that was ripe for the harvest.

In the book, *Jim & Casper Go to Church* Pastor Jim Henderson invites atheist Matt Casper to visit several churches with him to get an outsider's view of church practices. One of Casper's observations was that, without intending to, the church has become a closed society where people outside the Christian experience (the unchurched) find it difficult to fit in. [11]

Although his focus was on the shortcomings of the church as it attempts to attract seekers, Henderson illustrates the point that the church has, in fact, become a separate culture where people who don't adapt to the language, dress codes and social structure find themselves unable to fit in. And it appears that the more Christians become a part of this church culture, the less likely they are to reach out to non-Christians.

Interestingly, at the same time inner city pastors are addressing the reality that the African American church has lost sight of the main purpose of the church, another movement is being birthed from within the white suburban church. There is a trend now, in the suburban church toward a mission-focused, or missional ministry.

Over the last few years, I've attended seminars or discussion groups sponsored by these churches or by Bible colleges that have presented the concept of missional ministry. This new term; missional, was introduced to distinguish the ministry from a basic missionary concept and to contrast it from the current state of the church, which has been called the invitational or attractional church.[†]

Through this ministry; churches, Para-churches and individual believers are re-directing their efforts to restoring broken communities (read ghetto) through what Roxburg and Boren refer to as "engaging the context", or becoming part of the community in order to minister Christ to the community. The missional concept wrestles with the idea of re-defining the church in our rapidly changing world, and has given birth to what are being called; "intentional" neighborhoods, where suburban Christian families are intentionally relocating to the inner cities in order to become part of the community and to influence change in that community through living out the Christian example. By their own definition, Effective evangelism in the urban context, as in any other setting, requires that the Christian witness becomes immersed in the culture of the people they wish to reach.

The missional movement has certainly had its successes in creating viable solutions to the unique problems of under-resourced urban communities. Through this movement, community owned credit unions have been established, and many communities have seen the development of low cost housing as an outgrowth of their work. And intentional neighborhoods have had the effect of re-engineering racial demographics of the cities to create a more diverse population. But along with the desired effect of renewing the city through the engagement of the suburban Christian community also comes the not-so-desirable side effect of re-gentrification.

Re-gentrification (defined as the return of the gentry, or land owners) while improving the value of the property in a community, also causes an increase in the cost of services and goods, effectively forcing out those people who are least able to keep up with the rise in the cost of living - those people who are the focus of the effort.

While I commend the spirit of this effort in its attempt to establish a true sense of Christian community, there is the danger that it will be perceived as merely a reverse approach to the "white flight" that actually created much of the problem in the first place. And in a very real sense, perception can have a negative impact on the effectiveness of the missional ministry, because to a person living the ghetto reality perception is all that matters.

Although the intent may be to immerse themselves in the culture of the city in order to understand and identify with the urban experience; suburban whites can never really share that experience in its fullest sense, because they are aware (whether consciously or sub-consciously) that if the situation becomes unbearable, they have the option of leaving. In the perception of the person who is forced to live the ghetto experience, there will always be a certain amount of skepticism toward this type of experiment, because they know that they have no other recourse than to remain in the ghetto and try to find ways to cope with a never-ending series of insults, set-backs and disappointments.

Suburban churches are not alone in their passion to bring ministry help to the inner cities. At the national level, there are churches and para-church ministries from within the urban community that have responded to the call of the city. Organizations like the Christian Community Development Association founded by Rev. John Perkins, Pastor Eugene Rivers' Boston Ten Point Coalition, and the Urban Initiatives program of the Church of God in Christ headed by Bishop Edwin Bass have made great strides in addressing the challenges that confront our cities.

And while these organizations have begun great works toward meaningful ministry, they are but a few out of a multitude of organizations that have the capacity to help. And for all of the outreach efforts, whether within the urban or suburban church, few have taken the time to understand what is really needed, because the unspoken assumption is that—without asking or researching the root cause—they already know the solution to the problem.

This reminds me of an episode of the TV crime series, *Hill Street Blues* in which Detective Mick Belker (actor Bruce Weitz) has been assigned as a liaison to an actor who had been cast to portray a police detective in an upcoming movie. The actor is allowed to ride in the squad car, go on routine assignments and sit in on squad room activities in order to accurately capture the essence of what it means to be a detective in the tough city environment. As he begins to learn the mechanics of the police work, he also begins to mimic Belkers' character traits and affectations to the point of becoming an annoyance. Finally Belker, unable to take any more of the actor's behavior, explodes; "You don't just come down here and *know* me!"

It seems that everyone has a *vision* for the 'hood, and that somehow, without asking, listening and learning, we can just *come down here and know* what it means to minister to the needs of the inner city. But before any of us can minister effectively in the inner city, we must understand the underlying causes that produced the negative behavior and the violence; the reason behind the drug culture and the exploitative relationships; and—just as we would if we were preparing to minister in a foreign country—we must come to understand the unique cultural character of the 'hood and the circumstances that created and continue to perpetuate the urban experience.

CHAPTER TWO

A BRIEF HISTORY OF THE 'HOOD

For generations, people of good will have worked to remedy the difficulties that seem to be unique to the inner city. But with every generation the problems don't find resolution as much as they seem to find resurrection; and that with every change of political policy. I believe this is because, with every generation, we search for solutions to the symptoms rather than seeking to understand and address the causes that created them.

And while people outside of the urban experience may view the ghetto* as an amoral jungle or see its inhabitants as predators prone to violence, things were not always this way. In the inner cities of the past there was a sense of shared community and respect for the institutions of law, family and church even in the face of systemic racial discrimination.

From their beginning inner cities were populated by loving families, hard working parents, and respectful children who faced the future with hope whether they lived in conventional neighborhoods or in tenement housing. These were strong families with strong values. Not so much extended families, as families who extended themselves to embrace the entire community. Here every child, every weary traveler, and even the neighborhood drunk could find a hot meal or a helping hand because what little the people had, they had in common.

These were the communities where neighbors would pool their resources and sponsor rent parties to help others meet their monthly obligations. These were communities where children respectfully referred to adults as Mister or Miss, and every child knew that they had an obligation to excel in school because education was the universally accepted key to freedom.

In the ghetto of this era, there was a respect for life, for family and for God. So, the question arises; How could a people who survived the horrors of slavery, the ravages of racism and the emotional scars of segregation come to produce a generation that seems prone to self-destruction? To search for an answer, we start with the history of the inner city.

America's inner cities were created by a unique set of circumstances, most of which were precipitated by the racial climate of the times, beginning with a period historians call The Great Migration.

THE GREAT MIGRATION

In the years between 1870 and 1930 African Americans began leaving the indentured servitude of share-cropping in the south, and moved toward the promise of employment, respect and upward mobility of the industrialized north. By 1910 the Black population of cities like Washington, DC and New York, NY had increased to over 90,000 and in Baltimore, MD and Philadelphia, PA the numbers rose to 80,000. By 1920 the black population of Chicago had increased from 44,000 to 110,000 and Cleveland's population grew from 8,000 to 34,000.

This dramatic increase in the number of black city dwellers changed the cultural landscape of the north, but it also created an almost palpable animosity among whites. Where they had once dominated the workforce, whites now had to compete with blacks for semi-skilled factory jobs and limited housing.

As blacks migrated from the south, they found employment in the factories and stock yards of the major cities, but they also found a new form of racism in the north—de facto segregation in housing.

The National Housing Act of 1934, which was enacted to create affordable housing for struggling American families, had the effect (whether by design or by chance) of barring blacks from securing mortgage loans in predominantly white neighborhoods. Additionally, whites began forming "Neighborhood Improvement Associations" through which they could legally establish contractual agreements among white home-owners prohibiting the sale of their property to blacks. [1]

These restrictive covenants provided a way to circumvent anti-discrimination laws and added to the creation of heavily concentrated black urban settlements like New York's Harlem district, Philadelphia's Seventh Ward, Chicago's State Street or Baltimore's Druid Hill. Those wealthier or more prominent black families who were able to obtain property in white neighborhoods were threatened with bombings, arson or beatings and eventually were forced to flee the suburbs to become part of the overcrowded "exclusion-zones".

So for some, the inner-cities were just a more sophisticated version of the indentured servant's quarters of the south. For others, they were a refuge of safety from housing discrimination or the threat of white hostility.

The creation of this new urban ghetto brought about the birth of a new sub-culture with its own distinctive character. The evolution of black music from the Negro spiritual and Delta blues of the south to the urban styling's of be-bop and swing; the development of inner city style from down-home country to up-town cool; and even the transition from the southern drawl to the hep jive of urban colloquial speech expressed the new sophisticated soul of an emerging African American way of life. But this glib urban style only served to mask an unspoken awareness among blacks of the unique *otherness* of being African in America. And in this separate but unequal society, African Americans established their own social order; creating centers of commerce with businesses, banks, institutes of higher learning, and entertainment franchises with a focus on building equity and economic stability.

Great statesmen, business persons, inventors and artists emerged from America's inner cities. Poet and author, Langston Hughes; educator, Mary Mcleod Bethune; medical pioneer, Dr. Charles Drew; inventor,

Garrett Morgan and entrepreneur (and possibly the first female millionaire) Madame C. J. Walker were not the exceptions to the rule when it came to excellence, but were more a representation of the intellectual, artistic and business genius to come from Americas urban centers. And while the inner cities embraced their noteworthy, they also endured their notorious.

Sundown on Saturday would reveal the dimly lit honky-tonks, jook-joints and unspoken things done in the darkness—things that were kept hidden from polite black society. Here, the real-life characters of African American folklore, like "Stag-o-lee" Shelton; who became an urban legend by shooting Billy Lyons, or Frankie Baker; made famous in the tragic ballad of Frankie and Johnny, actually walked the dark alleys of the city. And if truth be told, many white suburbanites would find their way *across the tracks* to the Cotton Clubs and Speakeasy's of the ghetto to the sample the exotic and forbidden fruit of the Afrocentric experience.

At the core of urban civilization was the African American church. Giving birth, substance and purpose to almost every facet of urban life, the church became an institution in the black community. And black pastors, by default, became the conscience and sometimes the voice of an oppressed people.

During this era, the church carried such a reputation of integrity that Christian leaders, from the venerated pastors to the revered church mothers, commanded a respect that would cause the worst reprobate to stand erect, hide their dice or cigarettes and respond to a greeting with a "Ma'am" or a "Sir" ...but sadly, that reverence and respect would not last.

THERE AROSE ANOTHER GENERATION

"...and there arose another generation after them, which knew not the Lord, nor yet the works which he had done for Israel"

(Judges 2:10)

In a God-conscious society, even the ungodly have boundaries that they will not cross. But when a generation refuses to acknowledge God—or forgets Him altogether—there are no moral absolutes, guidelines or boundaries that must be respected. I'm convinced that this generational amnesia reached its height during the '60's.

Prolific writer and dear friend, Deborah L. Mason makes the observation that the generation of the '60's created an atmosphere of determined rebellion against conventional, true and God ordained principles and contributed to the downward spiral of society.[2]

Having grown up during those turbulent years, I have a slightly different perspective on the root causes of that "determined rebellion." This era came on the heels of the Eisenhower and Kennedy years, with its unspoken sense of well-being and hope for a brighter future. There seemed to be an innate sense that government could be trusted to do what was right and that its officials had the best interest of the people at heart. The rebellion that followed in the '60's wasn't necessarily the willful defiance of authority, as much as a reaction to the realization that our *Great Society* was only a mask that covered a racially biased system.

Communities of color had been promised their forty acres of the American Dream, but much like Lorraine Hansbury's metaphorical *Raisin in the Sun*, the deferral of the dream caused those communities to explode. The riots of the '60's were actually more of a delayed reaction than a willful defiance against the institutions of law and government. Much like the Los Angeles uprising of 1992 following the Rodney King beating, this was the cumulative effect of a people who had reached the point of ultimate frustration; outraged at being told for generations to wait for justice to arrive in its own sweet time. Whether one views this as ungodly rebellion, or a response to ungodly injustice, the aftermath was the same—violence, bloodshed and the loss of life.

The civil rights struggle of the '60's was not the first time blacks resisted unfair treatment in America. Historically, organized resistance dates back to the 1700's with the center of the resistance being the black church. Richard Allen and Absalom Jones, both ministers in the Methodist Episcopal Church, were among the first to boycott racial discrimination by withdrawing their membership from the segregated white church and forming the first African Methodist Episcopal church in 1791. They were followed in 1796 by the withdrawal of blacks from yet another segregationist church to form the African Methodist Episcopal Zion Church.

By 1892 Ida B. Wells had become the voice of black protest, as she launched her crusade against lynching and in 1905 W.E.B. Dubois convened a group of leaders in Canada to form the Niagara Movement, an association dedicated to aggressive action in the battle for equality.

But unlike the organized resistance of the past, the protests of the '60's marked the first division between the civil rights movement and the Christian church.

In the beginning, the marches, sit-ins and demonstrations were organized from within the church, as Christian ministers formed groups such as the Southern Christian Leadership Conference (SCLC), and the interracial Fellowship of Reconciliation (which went on to become the Congress on Racial Equality-CORE). Even some of the organizers of what came to be the more radical Student Nonviolent Coordinating Committee (SNCC) began as seminary students. And in the south, churches such as The Voice of Calvary, led by Rev. John Perkins actually suffered jailings and severe beatings as they stood on the front lines in the battle for equality.

With Christian activists at the forefront of the call to justice, the marches and demonstrations remained focused and non-violent. But when those non-violent protests were met with violence, the mood of the movement changed.

The murder of civil rights activist Medgar Evers, the deaths of four black girls in a Sunday morning church bombing, and the murder of three civil rights workers in Philadelphia, Mississippi were merely a prelude to the brutal attacks that were to follow. On April 4th 1968, the nation was rocked by the assassination of Martin Luther King, Jr. Almost immediately following the King assassination was the murder of Sen. Robert

Kennedy on June 5th. These events, coupled with a growing outcry against the Vietnam War brought about a nation-wide series of protest and marches. But these protests would be met with fierce and sometimes fatal responses.

In May of 1970, under President Nixon's "Law and Order" administration, unarmed students at Kent State University in Ohio were actually fired on by American forces as they marched in demonstration against the Viet Nam war. In a reaction to the Kent State Massacre (as it came to be called) students at the predominantly black Jackson State College in Mississippi began marching. This demonstration was also met with deadly force, as protesting students were shot and killed by local police.

The use of deadly force to control civic unrest and particularly to repress the march towards civil rights was not unique to this time period. In one of the most horrific times in the history of Africans in America, angry mobs of white Americans carried out one the most repressive acts of violence in U.S. history.

Between 1824 and 1951 there were over 300 events classified as "White Race Riots" in which white mobs attacked and destroyed entire black communities and murdered blacks by the hundreds.

From the inner cities of Chicago and East St. Louis, Illinois to the rural areas of Omaha, Nebraska and Greenwood, Oklahoma African Americans were dragged from their homes, shot, lynched or bludgeoned to death in broad daylight, with no intervention from government and with no legal repercussions for those whites who participated. The bloodiest and most concentrated of these race riots took place during the "Red Summer" of 1919 when blacks took up arms in self defense.[3]

The open hostility of angry white mobs in the 1920's seemed to be repeating itself in the violence of the 1960's. And just as they had done in 1919, blacks fought back. No longer willing to march peacefully while white mobs threatened violence and police loosed attack dogs on women and children, spokesmen like Stokely Carmichael and H. Rap Brown rose up to become the voice of an angry generation, and the focus of protest moved from a call to conciliation and equal rights to one of "Black Power."

As the tone of the movement became more intense and more immediate, younger groups became less patient with the idea of gradualism; or the process of gradual change. And in calling for peace and understanding with an increasingly hostile white America, the church's credibility as the voice of the civil rights struggle began to erode.

The strain that developed between the older more moderate Christian Pacifists and the new "Black Power" youth movement was intensified by the introduction of Marxist thought. Young college students were beginning to embrace the ideas of Karl Marx—that religion (perhaps, Christianity in particular) only served as an opiate to dull the senses to injustice. Additionally, the resurgence of the Nation of Islam with its fiery new spokesman, Malcolm X, brought negative attention to Christianity because of their view of the Negro Christian preacher as a hindrance to black freedom.[4]

As radical political power replaced Christian Pacifism as the most viable vehicle for black liberation, the church would grow silent on issues of race and resistance and retreat to the safety of evangelical preaching within the four walls of the sanctuary.

Rev. John Perkins describes the diluted role of the church during this period:

> Christianity was not seen as a force to change the situation, but as an emotional outlet to make it easier to endure... Black preachers had accepted this view of the church. Bible teaching, therefore, was considered secondary in most churches. What was important was

"good preaching" and "good preaching" meant preaching
that aroused the emotions and got people to shout.[5]

The concept of Christianity as a hindrance to freedom
or (more to the point) a tool of the white establishment
to diffuse anger and encourage the acceptance of
injustice, became the perception of the more radical
activists. And where the church had once been the
voice of freedom through leaders like Henry Highland
Garnett or Denmark Vesey who preached a gospel of
liberation while America still practiced slavery, now it
was regarded as little more than... an opiate.

As the Black Power generation of the '60's grew
older, the values that they passed on to their children
were different than the Christian ethics held by their
parents. The concept of church as the center of the
community had disappeared and children were no
longer directed to Sunday School or Bible study for
character development. The black pastor came to be
viewed more as a corruptible man than as a man of
God. And where the church and the minister had
been revered and respected, now they were disdained
or worse—ignored.

BLACK PRIDE

The ghetto of the 1970's saw some improvement,
as Job Core Programs and Urban Renewal projects

began to beautify the inner cities. A new era of black pride swept the ghetto, and James Brown captured the moment with his anthem; "Say it Loud; I'm Black and I'm Proud."

Once again, black businesses began to flourish and communities of color began to hope. But this time, the hope was not based in the American dream or in the Christian faith, as much as it was in the pride of Afro-centric identity and black self determination. Though still a presence, the church no longer commanded its position as the conscience of the community. Now the church shared its authority with the neighborhood Black Muslim Mosque, the Black Panther Headquarters or the local community center. Sunday Morning was no longer the domain of the Christian Church, when it could be taken for granted that almost every resident in the community would find their way to the sanctuary. Now, black families studied the teachings of Elijah Muhammad, Mao Tse Tung or searched for a sense of self in ancient African religions.

In many black households, observations of Christmas would be replaced by the African American Kwanzaa celebration. Even black preachers and businessmen would begin to wear conservative versions of the "Afro" hair style and the African dashiki to identify with their

African heritage. But this era of Black Pride would be short lived.

The conservative revolution of the Reagan years ushered in a period of political "backlash" that would virtually wipe out every gain made by blacks during the '60's and '70's. This wave of conservatism would also introduce an unusual change in the role the church would play in the civic and social arena.

THE REAGAN REVOLUTION

The decade of the '80's would introduce an era of conservative thought that would sweep the nation in politics, policies and even the pulpit, as Christian leaders would set the stage for change.

In 1979 Jerry Falwell, pastor of the Thomas Road Baptist Church of Lynchburg, Virginia began a personal crusade to exert his vision of conservative Christian influence in the political arena. Breaking a long standing rule in the Southern Baptist church of maintaining the separation of church and state, Falwell organized a conservative political action committee which quickly grew to upwards of four million members with at least two million active donors. With strong financial backing and the media platform that was already established with his own *Old Time Gospel Hour* telecast, Jerry Falwell was able to mobilize the southern white voters in such massive numbers that they became the largest conservative lobby in the United States.

The political influence of this *Moral Majority* actually shifted the political landscape of the nation, causing politicians to seek their endorsement for office. It was this political influence that swept Ronald Wilson Reagan into the oval office in 1980. And once in office, President Reagan began a series of the largest tax cuts in American history.

Depending on one's political viewpoint, Reagan's fiscally conservative *Supply Side Economics* either helped stimulate the economy by reducing taxes and removing government controls from big business (deregulation); or it marked the end of social welfare programs designed to help the poor and the cutting of federally funded programs that contributed to a dramatic increase in the homeless population during his administration.

From the urban perspective, Reagan's staunch refusal to acknowledge or meet with the Congressional Black Caucus and his lack of support for the enforcement of Civil Rights legislation sent an unmistakable message to marginalized people throughout the nation: the conservative revolution intended to end every entitlement program that had helped the poor and people of color. And as conservative fiscal policies and politics continued to favor the wealthy, the plight of the inner city intensified.

In his book *Malign Neglect: Race Crime and Punishment in America* Professor Michael Tonry lays the responsibility for the plight of urban America directly at the feet of the conservative administrations of the '80's.

According to Tonry, these administrations fought to reduce federal funding for those programs that had been designed to help the underprivileged, causing a seventy-five percent decrease in funds allocated to low-income housing programs. This disinvestment in the inner cities, for all intents and purposes, actually accelerated their deterioration and contributed to a reduction in the quality of public services [6]

The "Culture Wars" (a term coined by conservative activist, Patrick Buchannan) continued through both Bush administrations during the 1980's as more and more, conservative thought typified America's black population as a burden on society. This mind-set is expressed in the article *Constructing a 'Black-on-Black' Violence: The Conservative Discourse* by David Wilson of the University of Illinois.

Many statistics of social anarchy apply to the poor regardless of race. But crime and the fear of crime,

> drug and alcohol abuse, arson, vandalism, a dilapidated bombed-out physical environment and a way of life utterly separate from the American mainstream have become associated with poor city blacks more than any other group... The truth is we are up against the limits of public policy. At the heart of the disaster there is a vacuum of values. [7]

This *vacuum of values* perception portrayed inner city blacks as having no moral foundation and set the atmosphere for policies that would negatively impact the inner city throughout the '80's and '90's.

And as Falwell's Religious Right re-directed the political focus of America, another movement was taking hold in the church that would shift its focus from benevolence and civic responsibility to self-interest, and in some cases, self-indulgence.

THE NEW CHURCH

The Word/Faith movement signaled a shift in Christian thought as the new theology of Kenneth Hagin and Kenneth Copeland challenged the concepts of sacrificial charity and modest living as Christian virtues. Where Christianity had become synonymous with suffering and sacrifice, the new paradigm of Christian virtue became health, wealth and prosperity.

Based on E.W. Kenyon's *The Power of Positive Confession* and Napoleon Hill's *Think and Grow Rich* this new "name it and claim it" ideology captured the imagination of a new generation of Christians, and particularly black Christians.

Long tired of the theology of suffering that had been taught in so many black churches, African Americans began to embrace this new doctrine as a means of attaining the American Dream. This was a departure from the old "be content with such things as you have" mentality, and in the mind of many African American Christians, this was the passport to the affluent/ success-oriented lifestyles of their white Christian counterparts.

Whether or not one agrees with the doctrines of prosperity or positive confession, one truth is undeniable; the out-growth of this movement had a negative impact on the inner city.

No longer content to be identified with the poor and having found a new faith that equated salvation with success, many upwardly mobile blacks began to move their memberships to suburban white churches, taking their tithe and their talent with them. This new migration had the effect of all but stripping the inner city of its most vital resource-its earning class.

Many upper and upper-middle income families, educators, legitimate success models and community leaders fled the inner cities to find prosperity and acceptance in the suburbs. But in the aftermath of their leaving were the ruins of devalued property, blighted neighborhoods, the loss of pride in the community, and churches left without the financial resources to minister effectively.

As the housing laws of the 1930's created the inner city and the conservative political movement of the 1980's dismantled it's infrastructure, this new direction of the church made it acceptable for believers to disengage from the struggles of the community, preoccupied with their own prosperity. And still the final act that would transform the inner city into an urban nightmare of entrenched poverty, destabilized families and drug-related violence had not yet played out.

CRACK, CRIME AND THE WAR ON DRUGS

At the height of the Reagan Revolution, another sequence of events was unfolding that would unleash a wave of destruction in inner cities throughout the country.

At a 1979 symposium of scientists researching the use of cocaine in South America, experts discovered a dangerous new trend among users. In Lima Peru, cocaine processors had begun to smoke the paste residue left from the manufacturing of cocaine powder. This new method was found to produce extremely erratic behavior, dementia and psychosis. It was also found to be almost instantly addictive because it produced an intense but brief "high" with an immediate and depressing "crash", leaving the user craving another hit. According to these scientists; "There was a monster loose, a drug capable of totally enslaving its user." [8] By 1983, this *monster* found its way to the inner cities of North America.

In *Dark Alliance: The Story Behind The Crack Explosion*, a series of articles for the San Jose Mercury News, reporter Gary Webb exposed the link between a Colombian cocaine cartel and the inner city crack epidemic. Webb opens the series with this shocking revelation;

> For the better part of a decade, a San Francisco Bay Area drug ring sold tons of cocaine to the Crips and Bloods street gangs of Los Angeles and funneled millions in drug profits to a Latin American guerrilla army run by the U.S. Central Intelligence Agency. This drug network opened the first pipeline between Colombia's cocaine cartels and the black neighborhoods of Los Angeles... [9]

The crack explosion of the 1980's spread through America's inner cities like a plague, as the cartel tapped into the existing market for recreational drug use. Introducing the cheap, yet highly addictive drug, and then recruiting black neighborhood gangs as distributors had the multiple effect of concentrating the drug trade almost exclusively in the inner city, transforming common street gangs into a well-armed and sophisticated network and creating a generation of crack-addicts, crack-babies and- in the words of Congresswoman Maxine Waters;

> Wrecked lives and lost possibilities of so many people who got caught up in selling drugs, went to prison, ended up addicted, dead, or walking zombies from drugs. [10]

What followed in the wake of the crack explosion came in the guise of righteous indignation in response to the growing threat of violence in the inner cities. But it would ultimately prove to be a series of politically motivated policies and practices that would lead to an unprecedented number of minority arrests and convictions.

Following a daylight gun battle at Florida's Dadeland Mall in 1979, angry parents began to form organizations like the National Federation of Parents for Drug Free Youth, to combat teen drug use in their cities. During this same time period, the House Select

Committee on Narcotics Abuse and Control urged the president to take decisive action. [11]

THE WAR ON DRUGS

Promising a "Drug Free America" by 1995, President Reagan took the first steps toward what would become his War on Drugs. In January of 1982, Reagan initiated The Vice President's Task Force on South Florida, appointing George H. W. Bush as its director. This cabinet level task force combined the forces of the Drug Enforcement Administration (DEA), Federal Bureau of Investigation (FBI) and the Alcohol Tobacco and Firearms Divisions (ATF) giving them a broad range of authority to prosecute drug traffickers and suppliers. [12]

With the national focus on Florida, the drug cartels shifted their attention to New York and Los Angeles, confining their business almost exclusively to the inner cities. Pursuing the drug trade, Reagan created similar task forces across the country, making crack cocaine (and by default, the inner city) a prime target.

After the death of basketball star Len Bias in 1986, cocaine use became a charged issue and Reagan signed a bill that set aside millions to build new prisons with the intent of vigorously prosecuting drug traffickers. A provision of The Anti-Drug Abuse Act of 1986 called for mandatory minimum sentences for drug offenses. What made this sentencing peculiar was the difference in punishment for the offense. The minimum prison sentence for possession of 500 grams of powder cocaine—predominately in use in the white community—was set at five years. The same five-year minimum sentence was set for possession of 5 grams of crack cocaine, which was predominately in use in the black community (a ratio of 100-to-1). This sentencing disparity created an immediate increase in the arrest rate for people of color.

A study conducted by the Department of Psychology at Stanford University concluded that African American men, Latinos and women of all racial and ethnic groups were being incarcerated at a much higher rate than white men. The number of African American men rose from a rate of 3,544 per 100,00 in 1985 to a rate of 6,926 per 100,000 in 1995 and the number of Hispanic prisoners rose at a rate of 12 percent yearly.

The report went on to state;

> The increasingly disproportionate number of African American men who are being sent to prison seems to be related to the dramatic increase in the number of persons incarcerated for drug-related offenses, combined with the greater tendency to imprison Black drug offenders as

compared with their White counterparts. Thus, although Blacks and Whites use drugs at approximately the same rate, African Americans were arrested for drug offenses during the so-called war on drugs at a much higher rate than were Whites [13]

Also according to this data, of the arrests made few were for those who manufactured or imported drugs but eighty percent or more were for drug sales or possession.

Another, more disturbing implication in Reagan's drug war was the discovery that the government may have actually played a tacit role in the supplying of drugs to the inner cities, while at the same time conducting sweeping arrests of those caught in possession of the drugs.

If the 1989 report of the Congressional Subcommittee on Narcotics, Law Enforcement and Foreign Policy is accurate, the Reagan administration was not only aware of the Columbian cartel's cocaine pipeline to the inner cities, but actually undermined efforts to fight drug traffic in order to prevent interference with their political objectives in the region.[14] So, in a very real sense, while Reagan's War on Drugs apparently failed to end the drug trade, it succeeded in producing greater numbers of arrest and incarceration of blacks and Latinos.

Again, Tonry holds both the Reagan and Bush administrations accountable for the drug war's devastating effect on communities of color. He asserts that they actually had evidence that drug use was decreasing in the majority population, but that it was not decreasing in the inner cities. Simply stated, they knew the War on Drugs would be waged primarily in the inner cities and that those who would be detained, arrested and imprisoned would be predominantly blacks and Latinos. In Tonry's words; "The war's planners knew exactly what they were doing." [15]

In the wave of conservatism that came on the heels of the radical 60's and progressive 70's, it's understandable that there would be a certain amount of support for policies that would restore respect for Law and Order, at least from the conservative point of view. But for the obvious and deliberate focus on and arrest of the young black and Latino population, the question must be raised; Where were the voices of protest? Where was the call for equal justice under the law? In the *Land of the Free* and the *Home of the Brave*, why did no one speak out against this blatant attack against people of color?

THE POLITICS OF FEAR

As crime in the inner cities rose, the War on Drugs escalated the arrests rates of blacks and Latinos. In what has been referred to as *drug exceptions to the Bill of Rights*, the courts expanded the authority of law enforcement agencies to give the Justice Department the discretionary latitude to selectively stop, question and detain anyone who fit their description of a criminal type; to conduct aerial and electronic surveillance, random search and seizure and to monitor the mail of U. S. citizens, all without requiring a warrant. And in order to get the public to surrender these Fourth Amendment protections, people had to be convinced that the threat was real and immediate.

Throughout the history of the United States, people of color have not always been portrayed in the most flattering light. And since the emancipation of the slaves in 1863, black men in particular have been depicted as slow-witted or as sexual brutes; illiterate or conniving; docile or dangerous; depending on which description best served to justify the institution—be it slavery, segregation, employment discrimination or bias in the criminal justice system. The power to shape public opinion can be an extremely destructive weapon when it's used to malign a person or group.

The damage that is done can be far reaching and, in some cases, permanent.

In the media, from D. W. Griffith's *Birth of a Nation* to Quentin Tarrantino's *Django: Unchained* the character of African American men has been maligned, as being over-sexed, extremely violent and naturally prone to criminal behavior. In the area of psychological research, the idea of black men as inherently violent has been the subject of much study as America's *think-tank* produced such works as Thorsten Sellin's *The Negro Criminal* in 1928[16] and Guy B. Johnson's *The Negro and Crime* in 1941.[17]

Even today, negative portrayals in the media still associate blacks with crime, drugs, welfare fraud, teen pregnancy and dysfunctional families. And there are still psychologists who continue to produce studies to support the theory that blacks are, by nature, intellectually and morally inferior to whites. [18]

By the mid-eighties, this concept had become such a part of America's collective sub-conscious that the subject moved from hushed discussions around the office water cooler to the airwaves and written texts of the mainstream media. And through the media, these negative images contributed to the corporate idea of the black male as dangerous and inherently criminal.

This perception became so pervasive that even people who reject the idea of racism out of hand, found themselves affected by the fear of a black criminal underclass. To be fair, we have to acknowledge the fact that crime had increased in the inner cities as a direct repercussion of drugs and drug-related violence and that, in some instances, there was (is) even a fear of violent black men among blacks as well. But it is also a fact that as long as the violence was restricted to the ghetto, the crime and arrests didn't receive much media attention. It was only when the crime spread from the ghetto to the suburbs, that middle class whites began to fear for their safety and soon newspapers and magazines began to report muggings in New York's Central Park, home break-ins and robberies or attacks on joggers by marauding black or Latino gangs.

At this point, the news media recognized the value of reporting inner city crime and it seemed that the more sensational the story, the higher the viewer rating. And more often than not, when crimes involved drugs or violence, the picture displayed would be that of a young man of color either being arrested, arraigned or zipped into a body bag.

People were afraid and politicians weren't slow to recognize the benefit of the fear factor. Both

Conservative and Liberal alike began to pander to that fear, using the black criminal as a wedge issue to distinguish themselves from their opponents as "Tough on Crime."

Seizing this opportunity to bolster their ratings and to influence the political landscape, the popular media began to promote shock-jock talk-show personalities to agitate white middle class workers in support of conservative policies and politicians. And these charged diatribes have produced a racial polarity that has become more and more volatile and increasingly intolerant.

Even as recently as 2005, William Bennett, former Education Secretary of the Reagan administration, made this callous and racially charged remark on his *Morning in America* talk show;

> If you wanted to reduce crime, you could—if that were your sole purpose—you could abort every black baby in this country and your crime rate would go down.[19]

This type of sentiment, expressed in the national media, has added a distorted legitimacy to what, in the past would have been called exactly what it is—blatant racism.

And from Dr. Laura Schlessinger's unrepentant use of the *N-word* on her nationally syndicated show, and Don Imus' "Nappy Headed Ho's" reference to an African American women's basketball team to what has been referred to as Rush Limbaugh's "Top Ten Racist Quotes"[19], conservative talk show hosts have pressed their first amendment rights to use derogatory language in reference to African Americans with little or no effective protest or redress.

And no one would dare protest these racially insensitive comments, the disproportionate arrests, or the disparate sentencing because the public opinion had been manipulated to accept the reality that black men are criminal by nature, and need to be kept locked away from society.

In an article for salon.com, Maia Szalavitz describes the media's role in intensifying the anxiety over crack and crime, and the resulting impact on politics and the image of the black male.

> When it came to crack, the media escalated the panic and propelled a political arms race, in which Democrats and Republicans fought to outdo each other as anti-drug crusaders. The result was sentences for dealers and users that are longer than for rapists and even killers.
>
> In the end, crack did prove to be a long-term disaster for the inner city—not because of unending violence, but because of the resulting criminalization of young black men. [20]

The media creation of the "black criminal" as a universal symbol was all that was necessary to give the War on Drugs it's real and immediate threat. And in 1988 George Bush gave that threat a name.

WILLIE HORTON AND THE THREE STRIKES LAW

Willie Horton was a criminal. Without argument, Horton was a felon, a murderer and a rapist. And worse, Willie Horton was a black man. Typifying the racial stereotype that had been used to stigmatize black men for generations, Willie Horton was the face and the fact behind suburban white America's fear.

Willie was serving a life sentence without the possibility of parole for the murder of Joseph Fournier, a 17 year old gas station attendant. After robbing and stabbing the boy 19 times and leaving his body in a trash can, Horton had been arrested and, rightfully, sent to prison for life. But in an attempt to rehabilitate criminals, the government established a furlough program designed to help those who might be eligible for parole to re-enter society, seek employment and secure living quarters. It was during a weekend furlough that Willie Horton escaped custody and remained a fugitive for an entire year. In April of 1987 in Oxon Hill, Maryland, William R. Horton attacked and repeatedly raped a young white woman, stabbed her boyfriend, and attempted to escape in a stolen car.

Horton was arrested and sentenced to two consecutive life terms with eighty-five years added to ensure that he would never endanger the public again.

Willie Horton was a criminal and Willie Horton was a black man. And in 1988 George H. W. Bush used that image as a wedge issue in his campaign against Governor Michael Dukakis.

Promoting media "attack ads" designed to associate Dukakis with the Horton case, much as Reagan had used the image of "welfare queen" Linda Taylor to tie his opponent to alleged abuses of public assistance programs, won Bush a second term as a *tough on crime* President. But it also had the effect of making Willie Horton a national icon as suburban America's worst nightmare; a chronic black criminal, freed by a failed legal system. And by inference, every black man became suspect.

With the image of the violent black man firmly established in the public consciousness, anxiety gave way to anger as whites began to press government officials for protection from this perceived menace. And soon, compassion for the underprivileged became contempt for the unlawful; the concept of prison changed from rehabilitation to retribution, and the legal system began to reflect this trend.

In 1993, Washington State passed Initiative 593, the first in a series of laws designed to separate from society those felons deemed to be unresponsive to rehabilitation. California followed in 1994 with Proposition 184, with over 70 percent of the voters approving the measure. And by 2004, over 25 states had enacted similar laws. These new "Three Strikes" laws, like the drug war laws before them, imposed mandatory minimum sentences of twenty-five years to life without the possibility of parole and were originally intended to discourage repeat offenders from committing additional crimes, or to lock them permanently away.

The main focus of these laws were "career criminals" with three or more serious or violent felonies. But the application of the law soon expanded to include less serious crimes. Because of the impact of the War on Drugs, the possession of illegal substances became a felony and before long these non-violent offenses came to count as first, second and in many cases, third *strikes*. Now, people stopped in routine search and detain actions could be charged and sentenced to life in prison for possession of marijuana or common thieves could be sent away for life for shoplifting or for petty theft. And with drug sales taking place in the open on inner city streets, the easiest and most likely targets were African and Latino Americans.

The racial disparities in these arrests have resulted in a radically disproportionate number of African and Latino Americans incarcerated for drug offenses. Almost two-thirds of drug arrests result in convictions, which puts the incarceration rate at an estimated 67 percent of those arrested. And with blacks more likely than whites to be arrested on drug charges, the likelihood of their being incarcerated increases proportionally (or dis-proportionally).

A study conducted by the Human Rights Watch group came to this conclusion;

> Although the data in this backgrounder indicate that blacks represent about one-third of drug arrests, they constitute 46 percent of persons convicted of drug felonies in state courts. Among black defendants convicted of drug offenses 71 percent received sentences to incarceration in contrast to 63 percent of convicted white drug offenders. Human Rights Watch's analysis of prison admission data for 2003 revealed that relative to population, blacks are 10.1 times more likely than whites to be sent to prison for drug offenses.[21]

In *A Primer: Three Strikes- The Impact After More Than a Decade* the California Legislative Analyst's Office reported that African Americans make up more than one-third of the second and third strike felons, with Latino Americans at 33 percent, followed by whites at 26 percent. These disturbing figures place blacks at the highest level of felons serving mandatory life sentences at 37 percent, even though African Americans only make up 12 percent of the U.S. population. [22]

The obvious outgrowth of these massive arrests has been an overcrowding of state and federal prisons, leading to the privatizing of the correctional institutions and the creation of what has become a prison industry.

THE BUSINESS OF PRISONS

Today, privately owned prisons have become a business entity in their own right, generating jobs in construction, food services, weapons manufacturing, and security. But more unsettling is the fact that many states have legalized the contracting of prison labor, employing the inmate population at sub-minimum wage.

Prison corporations such as Wackenhut, Federal Prison Industries (a government-owned corporation using the trade name Unicor) or Oregon's Unigroup have contracted inmate labor to many U.S. corporations as a low-cost alternative to outsourcing the work to foreign countries. And the names of the corporations that use these services reads like a "Who's Who" of American industry, from national department stores and clothing manufacturers to information technology services[23]

One corporation's online advertisement boasts itself as the "Best Kept Secret in Contact Service" providing a nationwide network with over 1,700 experienced and college educated inmate agents (read prison inmates).[24]

In October of 2010, The San Francisco Chronicle detailed the deplorable treatment of inmates employed by prison corporations. According to the article, as of 2009 the recycling business alone employed over 850 inmates earning from 23 cents to $1.15 an hour while corporate profitability reached about 9.2 million dollars. [25]

With this type of revenue to be generated at such low costs, these corporations would seem to have a vested interest in massive arrests of poor people and, more so, in keeping them in prison for as long as possible. And when you consider the fact that such a large percentage of prison inmates –and particularly those serving life sentences– are people of color, it appears that prison industries have capitalized on the hopeless, the uneducated and the disenfranchised of the inner city who have fallen prey to the lure of the drug culture and have become the unwitting victims of the War on Drugs.

In my own ministry I have experienced yet another chilling reality as I have served in prison chapel outreach at jails and penitentiaries throughout Northern California.

Waiting at the kiosk to be cleared for entry at a local jail, I began to notice a trend as young mothers would bring their infants and toddlers along, standing in the long line to visit their husbands or boyfriends. As these children were being brought to jail on a regular basis, toys and a play area had been set up to accommodate them. My heart broke within me, as I realized that subconsciously, these children were being conditioned to accept prison as a normal part of their lives. The idea of jail would not be fearsome for them, and the threat of prison would not be a deterrent.

ARRESTED YOUTH

Today, black and Latino youth are arrested and held in detention facilities at alarmingly high numbers, and those numbers reflect the same racially disparate arrest rates of adults.

An article for the Annie E. Casey Foundation states that at least two-thirds of the disadvantaged youth held in detention centers are children of color. The article goes on to state that the increased use of juvenile detention over the past twenty years is due in great part to the increased rates of detention for African American and Latino youth.[26]

Some of these youth are guilty of no more than public order offenses (rowdy behavior) or breaking curfew. But others are guilty of acting out the culture of violence that has become the norm in their lives.

The United States is one of only a few nations that allows its' children to be sentenced to life in prison without the possibility of parole. And again, black youth are the recipients of harsher sentencing, receiving life without parole sentences at a rate of up to 10 times higher than white youth. In California, the ratio is 22.5 percent higher, with Pennsylvania sentencing Latino youth at ten times the rate of white youth.[27] In truth, inner city youth have become the perpetrators as well as the victims of violent behavior. From the prison-gang influenced dress and attitudes to the violence expressed in their video games and music, youth seem to have embraced a lethal lifestyle that has almost destined them to destruction.

Attending a symposium; "Communities Responding to Violence Among Youth", I was able to gain some insight into the root causes of this behavior.

Douglas Fort, a young man who was a product of the streets of East Palo Alto, California (once called the murder capital of the world) had been invited as a guest presenter. Fort had escaped the violence of the streets, and dedicated himself to helping other young people.

In his presentation Fort described in stark detail, a major cause for the negative behavior among urban youth... anger.

Among young people between the ages of 14 and 25, he explained, the anger is a direct result of a sense of abandonment. Youth of this age group harbored an unspoken anger with the fathers who had abandoned them. Fathers who were either willfully absent from their children's lives (irresponsible "baby-daddies") either uncaring or unwilling to accept their roles as providers and protectors, or those fathers who had been forcibly removed from their families by the criminal justice system.

Fort went on to describe yet another group of angry youth. These were the children between the ages of 8 and 14 who had been abandoned by both father and mother. The mothers of this age group were absent because of substance addictions, destructive romantic relationships, or again, incarceration. Not only has this sense of being abandoned created a latent anger among inner city young people, it has also left them prey to every pimp, street hustler and drug dealer as well as every prison corporation looking to benefit from their angry behavior.

And as this climate of anger and violence intensifies, more young people are being murdered in drive-by shootings; some even on the steps of the neighborhood church. And increasingly more innocent young people are dying at the hands of over-zealous police officers, killed during routine arrests for fear of concealed weapons or resisting arrest with no one but their families to decry the injustice.

THIS IS THE WHY

From the creation of the inner city in the 1930"s to it's subsequent destabilization and degeneration into the urban *war zone* we know today, the history of the 'hood has played out like a symbiotic cycle of destruction with each successive problem deriving it's existence from the one before it. Discriminatory policies creating the poverty; poverty feeding the hopelessness; hopelessness feeding the substance abuse; substance abuse breeding violence and fear; and violence and fear feeding discriminatory policies... and the cycle continues.

The erosion of confidence in government and in the church; the deliberate marginalization and disenfranchisement of people of color; housing discrimination and the elimination of federal assistance for the underprivileged; the abandonment of our children and an increasingly disconnected and dispassionate church have all become a part of the cycle that feeds the deteriorating enclave that we have come to know as the 'hood.

It's no small wonder, after generations of such prejudicial practices and policies, that blacks, Latino's and the marginalized community have developed an oppositional counter-culture with it's own distinct language, ethos and defiant ghetto swagger, embracing a self-affirming cultural stereotype. This is their way of rejecting the society they believe has rejected them.

A dear friend of mine would use the phrase;

"Esto es el por que" – This is the "why".

This is the *why* behind the violence and the vandalism. This is the *why* behind the abusive relationships and self-destructive behavior. This is the *why* behind the attitude and the anger.

And this... this is the *why* that the church is called to address. This is the purpose and the passion of the gospel; to "go quickly into the streets and the lanes of the city". This is our conviction and our calling; to go *through* our Samaria rather than around it for the sake of the one soul at the well.

Just as we would study a foreign culture in order to understand its people, history and their way of life before we attempted to reach them with the gospel, we must take the same respectful approach to inner city evangelism. And when we have a better understanding of the causes that created and continue to perpetuate the inner city experience, we will be better able to develop a more informed strategy on how to reach the 'hood for Jesus.

CHAPTER THREE

WE WRESTLE NOT

"For we wrestle not against flesh and blood, but against powers, against the rulers of the darkness of this world, against spiritual wickedness in high places."

Ephesians 6:12

A s we become more informed in the area of inner city dynamics, we are better able to reach the people in the cities. But even with that information, there are greater issues and influences that we must contend with.

Over the last several years, Christianity has come under intense scrutiny—if not outright attack—as a result of the changing moral landscape of what some have come to call *Post-Christian* America.

From challenges to the authenticity and authorship of the Bible to legal challenges to re-define marriage in renouncing the biblical definition, the Christian witness has become the focus of pointed and sometimes, hostile criticism.

Adding to the problem of post-Christian and sometimes, anti-Christian thought is a disturbing trend that has taken root within the Household of Faith. As cultural politics and media manipulation have added to the climate of fear and distrust between classes and cultures, many professing Christians have been persuaded by this influence and have begun to separate themselves from the undesirable underclass of the inner cities.

These *undesirables*; the prostitutes, the drug dealers and the adolescents whose behavior, dress and choice of music offend us are the outsiders who refuse to fit into the image of our Western Christian culture. So, we excuse ourselves from engaging them, sharing the gospel with them or inviting them into our churches. Without realizing or intending to, we have unwittingly built a not-so-invisible wall between us and the very people that Jesus came to reach.

"For the Son of man is come to seek and to save that which was lost"

Luke 19:10

And I say not so invisible because sometimes we, in the church, have a way of making the *unchurched* feel unwanted, and even undesirables can sense when they're not welcome.

It seems that in our attempts to reach the world with the message of salvation, in many instances, we have become guilty of trying to reform society into our cultural image—the way we dress, act and interact—in essence, making Christianity a cultural expression more than a commitment to follow the Christ. And in coming out from among them, we have separated ourselves as the church *against* them and cast them as the enemies of God.

We have allowed ourselves to be drawn into a cultural confrontation; making a division between those we have deemed acceptable and those we have segregated as undesirable. In doing this, we separate ourselves, not only from the ungodly elements of sin, but from the victims of poverty and injustice. And in stigmatizing those who have devalued their own lives as the result of societal, emotional or physical abuse, we have inadvertently hurt the cause of Christian evangelism by making the Faith appear to be our own private war... us against them.

And in separating ourselves against them, we make the unspoken statement that we esteem ourselves as more godly than them, only serving to further alienate ourselves from them.

I was teaching at a symposium on community outreach that had the theme *Tearing Down the Walls/ Building Bridges*, and asked the obvious question; "Who built the walls?" After some discussion, the consensus of the class was that we in the church had built them, creating the division between our ministry and our mission field. Our mission field is the people outside our *walls*; souls who secretly yearn for a sense of fellowship and belonging, who really want to live more fulfilling lives, and who really want to know the love of Christ. They just need to be convinced that someone genuinely cares for and about them.

When we fail to reach beyond our walls and look past the outward appearance of the individual to see the inner person and their inner brokenness, we miss altogether the reason for Jesus' coming.

"The Spirit of the Lord is upon me, because he hath anointed me to preach the gospel to the poor; he hath sent me to heal the brokenhearted, to preach deliverance to the captives, and recovering of sight to the blind, to set at liberty them that are bruised, to preach the acceptable year of the Lord."

Luke 4:18,19

The poor—not just financially, but spiritually poor; without hope and without means. The brokenhearted—whose lives have been devastated by disappointment or divorce. The captives—who are in bondage; emotionally, mentally and spiritually, bound by addictions to alcohol, drugs or sex. The blind—both physically and spiritually; who cannot, and sometimes, *will not* see. The bruised—battered by the storms of life; abusive relationships, hatred, discrimination and despair. These are the focus of Jesus' ministry, these are the ones He chose to live and die for. And these are the ones we have aligned ourselves against as adversaries in a war of cultures.

Almost as if to emphasize this point, the media has reported on churches that have set up picket lines to protest the burial of an avowed homosexual; professing Christians who have bombed abortion clinics; and angry Christians publicly burning copies of the Qur'an and campaigning against the construction of Muslim Mosques in communities that were once were considered Christian strongholds. These acts of aggression in the name of the Faith have caused Christianity to be viewed as a religion of narrow-minded bigots, of the ignorant and unlearned, and of people who find it easier to hate than to try to understand and tolerate the beliefs of others.

I am not suggesting that the church change its position on fundamental issues of the Faith, but that we remember that the Bible's Great Commission is a charge to win a soul... not a culture war.

In striving against social classes and sub-cultures, we have only succeeded in driving a wedge between the churched and the unchurched and have added momentum to the growing anti-Christian sentiment already at work in the world. And because they are very aware of our walls, many of those that we have rejected have now rejected us, and have taken up arms (philosophically and in some instances, physically) in defense against what they see as an effort to impose Christian rule in America.

A visit to any one of the many internet chat rooms dedicated to cultural or religious diversity will reveal a growing animosity toward both Christianity and the Christian. In these "blogs", the challenges have become pointed and sometimes, personal. Here, I've paraphrased a random sampling from some of the web sites I visited.

- Everyone has a right to believe whatever they choose, no matter how irrational. But they don't have the right to impose their beliefs on others.

- Why can't you let gay people live their lives as equals among us?

- We Native Americans were taken from our traditional homelands in the name of Manifest Destiny. Your "god" gave you the right to decimate our people, for your own benefit. You enslaved us to work in your missions, where your diseases ravaged our bodies.

All of this in the name of your "god". That doesn't sound very Christ-like to me.

- Why follow some white mans Bible that was used to keep our grandmothers and fathers in slavery?

These were among the more tame entries on the web, but they all expressed a deep seated anger (some, even outright hatred) in response to Christianity and the Christian witness.

I experienced some of this anger first-hand at an outreach rally in San Francisco. On a street corner not far from City Hall, I watched as people whose lives had been utterly destroyed by substance abuse, poverty and hopelessness sat on the curbs and the walkways that led to the rotunda. I saw the brokenness in their faces, as they were reduced to asking for hand-outs of food or spare change just to survive for the day. I noticed a gathering of young men who had chosen an alternate-sex lifestyle, and could see the emptiness in their eyes as their ill-fitting wigs hung loosely over their own dirty and matted hair. It wasn't their lifestyle or appearance that shook me. What did amaze me, however, was the anger they expressed when I merely offered them a tract and an invitation to visit the sponsor church.

One or two made it a point to get my attention, in order to visibly demonstrate their disdain. Another accepted the tract, but tried to engage me in a debate over my own *you-a-mess* (his words) condition to signify that I had no right to share the gospel with him... or with anyone else, for that matter.

I was somewhat heart-broken, not because of the rejection, but as I stood there, a younger group of boys paraded by and it was plain that I was watching one generation who had sacrificed their lives on the altar of sexual pleasure, and the next, determined to follow in their footsteps. They were young, they still had a future, and they were oblivious to the destructive end-result of those choices being lived out right in front of their eyes.

Increasingly, those who have not embraced the Faith, those who reject the Faith, and those who engage in alternate lifestyles have become vehemently and overtly angry with the Christian witness. Not only do they reject the message of salvation, they seem adamant about their right to reject the messenger as hateful and judgmental... even to their own destruction.

On a recent late night talk show, the subject of judgmental Christianity took center stage, as the celebrity host invited a preacher who had been dis-fellowshipped (ex-communicated) to share his new message of inclusivity. His dismissal from a mainstream denomination came as the direct result of his introduction of the idea that all humanity is already "saved", regardless of lifestyle, faith or a lack of faith. According to his message, mankind is not lost, but simply unaware of their salvation and need only to be informed, so that they can enjoy the benefit. Actually, this is not a new concept, but was introduced as a speculative question on universal salvation by first century writers Clement and Origen between 195 and 225 A.D. Their argument was that, perhaps, after a period of punishment in purgatory, all humanity might be reconciled to God and still enjoy the blessings of Heaven[1]

As the pastor (who has since, founded an expansive ministry) continued to share his new *revelation*, the host made no attempt at hiding her disdain for what she considered to be a judgmental church that had the audacity to condemn sin. She gave her blessing to the pastor and encouraged him that he was one of the few who "got it right"

The danger here, is not as much the introduction of erroneous doctrine, as the idea that public opinion; moreover, public celebrity, has the right to determine what is or what is not the message of the gospel. Worse yet is that those who are influenced by celebrity opinion will be misled into a false gospel, while those who declare the truth will be marginalized as narrow-minded, bigoted and judgmental. And now that Christianity has come to be associated more with prosperity and partisanship than with practice, more non-Christians have come to view the Faith with a greater degree of skepticism than in times past.

THE CHALLENGE OF CHANGE

As the world outside the church has changed in the way it views Christianity, many within the Body have changed in the way we view ourselves... and our ministries.

As a rule, I advocate for change when that change is required to meet the needs of our changing communities. Of itself, change is not necessarily negative, neither is change foreign to the church, when you consider the history. Over the centuries, our churches have changed and adapted to changes in world governments and to changes generated by new revelations of biblical understanding. In 313 A.D. Christian worship was moved from the hidden caves and catacombs to the great cathedrals as the Edict of Milan re-structured the relationship between church and state, making Christianity an officially recognized religion in the Roman Empire. Again, in 1517 A.D. Martin Luther ushered in a new era of understanding through his Protestant Reformation, re-introducing the concept of salvation by Grace alone.

In U. S. history, the church adapted to the changes in America's economic infrastructure. In the early years of the agricultural era, the church produced "Circuit Riders", those preachers who would travel from region to region, planting and pastoring multiple churches in rural settings. As the Industrial Revolution of the 1780's brought in centrally located textile mills, factories and foundries, modern cities sprang up around them, and the church changed, becoming the cornerstone of the community. And now, as the Age of Technology has created a global economy based on the exchange of information, the church has adapted once more by harnessing the power of that technology to offer live streaming internet broadcasts of worship services, provide on-demand sermons and present on-line Bible studies complete with printable materials.

The church has indeed risen to the challenge of change, possibly more now than at any other time in history. From the new "Seeker-Friendly" services to bilingual and multi-cultural ministries, and from traditional worship celebrations to "Holy Hip-Hop" youth rallies, the church has adapted its methodology to meet the changing needs of a changing society.

Again, I do agree with change where change is needed. But there is an inherent danger when that change carries with it the potential to corrupt sound biblical doctrine; when attempts at changing our method brings about a change in our message.

Over a period of the last thirty years, the church has witnessed a subtle shift, as the focus of the ministry and the content of the message has been gradually re-directed from the gospel of salvation to the gospel of self-empowerment. Sundays subject matter has changed from the power of the Word to transform our lives to the power within our words to create the lives we choose. We have come to the place where we equate the Abundant Life with the accumulation of wealth, and our faith that God can do "exceeding abundantly above all that we ask or think" has been replaced with our ability to create our own reality through visualization, positive mental imaging and positive confession. A close examination of these new doctrines will reveal that they have more basis in New Age philosophy than in the New Testament Theology.

The principles taught in books like *Self Empowerment and the Subconscious Mind* by Carl Weschcke and Joe H. Slate [2] or *Money and the Laws of Attraction* by Esther and Jerry Hicks [3] promote an ideology that places the human mind in the realm of the supernatural, equating our ability to imagine with God's ability to create; in a manner of speaking, making us co-creators with the Divine. And this popular thought has crept into our churches, teaching that we can actually learn to attract wealth, health and prosperity through the things that we discipline ourselves to think.

Admittedly, the messages of self-realization, fulfilling our potential and increasing our financial wealth can be appealing, especially to someone who may have occupied the lowest rung of the social or economic ladder for most of their lives. It is encouraging to know that God believes in us and wants the best for us. And as we review the works of the health wealth and prosperity teachers, we find their message very empowering and compelling. The deceptive turn from doctrinal soundness comes into play, however, when that message moves into the methodology of their doctrine.

In his New York Times best seller *Your Best Life Now*, Pastor Joel Osteen encourages us to develop a healthy self image, to "discover the power of your thoughts and words" and to be mindful that we are in fact *choosing the right thoughts*. In explaining how this works, Osteen shares with us "Just like a magnet, you will attract what you continually think about" [4]

This application of training our thoughts in order to draw those things to us that we desire is the same principle taken from in the "Laws of Attraction", as described in the New Age best seller *The Secret*

> *"Nothing can come into your experience unless you summon it through persistent thought."* [5]

According to this belief, the means of attaining all that we want almost always revolves around our ability to speak or think those things that favor our desires until they miraculously manifest themselves. And by this practice, we take God's sovereign will out of the equation and focus continually on our own fulfillment in order to satisfy our personal desires. It appears that the only difference between the prosperity doctrine and the Laws of Attraction is that the New Age philosophy sees God as an impersonal concept, rather than a personal Deity. Both use personal testimonies and stories of successful applications of the principle. Both use references to God's plan for our increase. And both use the power of the human mind and positive confession to create the desired reality

I will say again that, at the first reading, the health, wealth and prosperity doctrine can be appealing and attractive because it affirms God's love for us, and encourages us that He wants us to have everything that we desire. And all we have to do is discipline ourselves to think the proper thoughts—those thoughts that bring wealth and happiness; those thoughts that attract the right types of people into our lives; those thoughts that reject poverty and suffering.

But in embracing this school of thought, we have come to a place where our priorities are guided by our appetites and our desires, and the emphasis in our message has changed from personal salvation to personal gain. Gone, are the testimonies of lives transformed by the power of the gospel and of miraculous healing through faith in God's Word. Salvation and servanthood have been sacrificed on the altar of self-empowerment and self-gratification, and the call to readiness in the church has changed from, "Maranatha, our Lord cometh" to the call of the covetous... "Money, cometh."

While this book is not intended as a study in comparative religions or New Age philosophy, we must recognize the impact that this re-direction of our message has had. In following this trend, we have lost sight of the true message of the Bible and we have forgotten that this gospel is not a vehicle for financial gain or personal prosperity.

In 1 Timothy 6:3-6, the Bible is explicit about equating gain with godliness, and warns us against those that err, "supposing that gain is godliness ... but godliness with contentment is great gain."

THE MEASURE OF SUCCESS

This change in our message and ministry may well have had its beginnings in another change that took place some years earlier, when our concept of success in ministry was re-defined.

The phenomenal success of the Yoida Full Gospel Church of Seoul, Korea set a new standard for the church, creating the most successful model of what has come to be known as the Mega-Church (defined as protestant churches with regular weekly attendance of 2,000 or more) Using a strategy of door to door invitational evangelism and developing cell-type home Bible study groups, Pastor David (aka Paul) Yongghi Cho challenged the concept of the modest neighborhood church, creating a church built on a corporate model, with enough influence to secure the nearby island of Yeouido, where they built a new ten thousand seat sanctuary. Based on the success of the Yoida church, Cho founded his Church Growth International organization with a mission to teach his evangelism and church growth techniques to pastors and church leaders throughout the world.

In building his mega-church and his training ministry, and establishing himself as an authority on church growth, Cho re-defined the concept of successful ministry as others began to emulate his success by applying his techniques. This brought in a new era in ministry, as those who were able began their own mega-church ministries, erecting massive buildings or purchasing sports stadiums to accommodate the tens of thousands who would attend their worship services.

Soon, the success of a ministry would not be measured by Gods anointing or the lives of those who were transformed or the homeless who were housed or the hungry who were fed. The measure of success would become the number of people who attended, their economic status and the level of prestige that the Pastor and/or the church had attained.

Seizing this trend, public relations consultants began to develop marketing strategies for churches and for pastors. From the viewpoint of the more prominent Christian marketing firms, church ministry has become an industry with a marketable product. Pastors, preachers and worship leaders have become commodities to be wrapped in attractive packaging and branded for maximum market saturation and the message of their ministries has been tailored to appeal to the broadest possible audience. In this new ministry model, the focus has shifted from winning a soul, to competing for a market share where increase in church membership equates to increase in revenue.

In a practical sense, a public relations department can actually be an asset to a church or a ministry. Direct-mail canvassing campaigns with attractive printed materials can serve as an effective tool to make the neighborhood aware of the programs and services offered by the church, or of a sermon series that may be of particular interest in meeting their needs. In many ways, evangelism can be tied to the concept of marketing, as it relates to gaining an understanding of the people we want to reach and the most effective ways to reach them. Applying some of the principles used in marketing can help put the message of the gospel into a context that can be more readily received, and marketing research can help us define and better understand the actual needs of the communities we are called to serve.

But in allowing independent marketing firms to package and produce our ministries, we have allowed ourselves to be re-fashioned into a professionally choreographed *stage performance* with the same message, the same focus and, many times, with the same speakers traveling from one mega-conference to the next.

Individuality in presentation and uniqueness of the anointing and calling have been lost, as those who want to promote their ministries begin to imitate those who are the most popular or financially successful. The biblical principle of the five-fold ministry of the church, as described in 1 Corinthians chapter 12 and Ephesians chapter 4 (with each ministry gift serving a unique and separate purpose) has been undermined by the popularity driven event-ministry that would entertain rather than exhort and soothe rather than stir to action. And in seeking popularity, we have lost our prophetic voice; the ability and responsibility to take the unpopular stand in speaking out against ungodliness in individuals and institutions.

Another outgrowth of this trend has been the creation of celebrity preachers and Christian entertainers whose extravagant lifestyles have drawn both public and government scrutiny in the use (and sometimes, misuse) of their donations and funding. These excesses have cost the Christian witness in terms of integrity and credibility. For the Christian, credibility is not measured in what we say, but in what we do, and *street credibility*—the way we are viewed by our community—is the integral part of urban evangelism that will validate or invalidate our witness.

If we are going to be effective in winning the city, we must realize that the greatest weapon in our evangelistic arsenal is not the public relations department, the staged events or the slick ad campaigns—and I will admit that these promotions do serve to attract those who are already inclined to attend church. But those who are on the outside of the church are watching what we do and are judging our faith by the lives we live.

As a part of my personal evangelism strategy, I've developed the practice of greeting the *brutha's* on the street as I leave the sanctuary after service. My intent is to open the opportunity for future dialogue to share the gospel and, hopefully, to break down the barriers between the street corner and the *amen corner.* Many times I'll get a nod or even a smile, letting me know that they are appreciative of the fact that someone from within the church is reaching out to them. But on one occasion, the response wasn't as favorable.

On this Sunday, I was dressed in my full clergy attire —black suit, black shirt, white banded clerical collar— for all intents and purposes, looking the part of a godly preacher. As I gave my usual greeting to a young man on the street, he responded with "Whassup, player?"

The real meaning of his statement didn't dawn on me until I was in my car driving home. The young man recognized by my attire, that I am a clergyman, but his statement placed me in the category of being a *player*. A player, a pimp, a predator, a user—someone who makes a living by taking advantage of the weak or the gullible. As I reflected on the moment, I wanted to get angry with the man for what I took as an act of extreme disrespect, not only toward me, but toward the ministry. But then I realized something; he wasn't addressing me as an individual, he was addressing me according to his perception of all preachers as predators who take advantage of the weak and the gullible for personal gain. And the reality is that among many of the young men in the street, this perception is common, and in some cases... not without merit.

From the fall of national television evangelists in the '70's to the sex and financial scandals involving today's' church leaders, all of which have been played out in the media, the physical church (and I make a separation between the organized entity established by men and the biblical church that Jesus established *within* men) has lost much of it's integrity and it's believability. And while we convene private councils and hold press conferences to control the damage to our credibility, those outside the Household of Faith have weighed our churches in the balance, and found us lacking.

If we are going to reach the streets of our city, we must restore our credibility. And if we are going to restore our credibility, we must realize this truth;

Before the world can see the Jesus in the Bible, they must see the Jesus in us.

And so, we built the walls; Christians judging the unchurched as undesirable, and those outside of the church judging the Christian as judgmental and hypocritical. As a baptized Body of Believers, we cannot allow ourselves to be deluded into the belief that God is at war with sinners. In fact, to the contrary; the Bible teaches that God commended his love toward us, in that while we were sinners, Christ died for us. Romans 5:8 (paraphrase mine).

Our purpose in sharing the gospel is not to fight against, but to reach out to every segment of lost society; the broken, the poor, the hurting, the spiritually blind, the outcast and the undesirable. Our calling is to exemplify the Risen Savior in our lives and lifestyles and to reveal the life-changing power of the gospel in the miracle of our transformed lives; lives that are testimonies of His power to change undesirables (such as we were) into the image of His likeness.

And if we are going to reach them, we must also realize that we are not in contention with them, but against the forces, both natural and spiritual, that oppress them and create the circumstances that keep them from abundant life in Christ Jesus.

Our contention, if we must contend, is to re-capture the message of the gospel as it was originally intended, to re-focus and re-direct our ministries to the extent that every functioning auxiliary in the church or outside the walls of the church is a conduit to salvation, and to re-commit ourselves as a church and as individuals to the ministry of reconciliation.

CHAPTER FOUR

THE FAITH WHICH WAS ONCE

"Beloved, when I gave all diligence to write unto you of the
common salvation, it was needful for me to write unto you,
and exhort you that ye should earnestly contend for the
faith which was once delivered to the saints"

Jude 3

In Jude's letter to the church, he finds it necessary to encourage them that they must earnestly contend for the principles upon which the Faith had been established; literally to fight to preserve the Faith, as it was originally intended. Apparently, there was a danger of their losing sight of the message and the mission. Perhaps, over a period of time there was the potential for a compromising of the standards that had been set, or the chance that erroneous doctrine might creep in, subverting the fundamental truths which were the foundation of the church.

Throughout the Bible there are warnings against false teachers who would somehow find their way into the heart of the church and establish themselves as leaders; only to compromise our faith and mislead the unwary. The Apostles Peter and John add their voices to Jude in warning against those "deceivers" who had "crept in unawares." These, they warned, would bring heretical teachings into the church that would cause the way of the truth to be misrepresented and the message of the gospel to be obscured.

In the book *Jim & Casper Go To Church*, atheist Matt Casper shares an unsettling insight, when he makes this observation about the mixed messages he receives when he visits our churches.

> [either] The church's mission is to plant more churches, or the churches mission is to help those in need, or the church's mission is to make people into millionaires- or at least to promise to- and make the church leaders millionaires in the process. [1]

The message of the church, as Casper puts it, is "all over the place." Is this the message and the mission that God intended for the church? What was the Faith as it was once delivered; and have we moved away from those foundational teachings?

THE FIRST CHURCH

Investigating the practices of the first Christians and the early church yields some interesting contrasts between what was and what is now considered the Christian Church. The church of the first century was, in many ways, radically different from what we have become accustomed to and might more aptly be described as a commune than the conventional church of today.

The church of Jesus' day was a community of believers who shared everything with one another, according to Acts 2:42-45. First century historian Justin Martyr writes that those who had in the past, placed their affections on the accumulation of wealth and possessions willingly brought everything that they owned and placed it in the common collective to be shared equally with everyone who had need. [2]

The Christians of this era shared in doctrine, in faith and in the "breaking of bread, and in prayers." They embraced a lifestyle free from every sinful practice and were known for their humility, charity and their love for one another. In the early church, there were no written gospels, only the collected Scriptures of Moses and the Prophets. So, their Christianity was based in the fact that many of them had first-hand experience with the Messiah, or they had been taught by those Apostles or Disciples who had been with Him.

Their faith was based on eyewitness information that was commonly known in their life time. In Galatians 3:1 we find that the knowledge of Jesus Christ; crucified and resurrected, had been made evident among the people. The Apostle Peter also attests to having been one among many eyewitnesses of the resurrection, as were the rest of the disciples and over five hundred others, some of whom were still living as the gospel accounts were being written. So faith in Jesus as the Christ of God—though a departure from the conventional religious belief of that time—was an undeniable fact in the minds of the early Christians.

Because of this unshakable belief, the leaders of the church also exercised power and authority in the Name of the Risen Savior. Not in their mighty words or eloquent speech, but they were able to manifest the power of God through demonstrations of the Holy Spirit.

The Apostles drew attention to salvation through Jesus by their prophetic revelations and the miracles that they performed in His Name. And because of this, the witness of the church was effective beyond their meager numbers, as they evangelized with signs of healing and deliverance that supported their claim that the Messiah had indeed come.

Whether or not one agrees with demonstrative expressions of faith, the indwelling power of the Holy Spirit in the believer or the manifestations of miracles in the church, the fact remains that this was the vehicle that God used to empower the witness of His church.

The power of God's Spirit at work in the church was also attested to by first century historian, Irenaeus.

> For after our Lord rose from the dead, the Apostles were energized with power from on high when the Holy Spirit came down. They were completely filled and had perfect knowledge. [3]

Not only were the leaders of the church empowered, but many of the lay membership exhibited that same authority in various expressions. The ministry of the church, as described in chapter 11 of 1 Corinthians, was likened to a physical body with eyes, ears, hands and feet, all individual units working in harmony for the strengthening of the body as a whole.

In the church of this era, there were no divisions in the leadership or in the Body, as every gift—whether natural or spiritual—was appreciated and recognized as a meaningful part of the whole ministry. Each person and each gift was engaged for the benefit of the whole. So, while there was an established chain of accountability within the ministry of the church, it was not unusual to see the gifts of the Spirit in operation throughout the Body.

The church of this day was not a wealthy one, nor was its focus on raising money, but because of the manifestation of the power that had indwelt them, they managed to turn the world "upside down", converting entire communities, cultures and continents within the first one hundred years of their existence.

Another contrast was in the early church's commitment to stand for the Faith in speaking truth to power. Contrary to the popular view of a docile and compliant church, this group was radical in their commitment to the Savior; not in unlawful demonstrations or rowdy behavior, but in their courage and boldness in taking a stand for the gospel at the cost of their freedom... and sometimes their lives.

Author Mark Guy Pearse writes:

> Within a week of Pentecost, the leaders of Christianity were in prison, and refused to give any promise to the authorities that they would recognize any law which was contrary to the commandment of God. [4]

This church was willing to go to prison or to die as martyrs for their convictions. They preached openly and boldly, they witnessed with authority, they were of one mind and of one faith. And they, through their love of God and for people, put their lives and belongings at risk; allowed themselves to be tortured; sawn in half; fed to wild beasts; hurled to their deaths; stoned or hanged upside down for the testimony of Jesus Christ. And in so doing they changed the course of the world.

Through the transitions in governments and society, the church has adapted and changed. As the original Apostles were martyred, and the first generation of eyewitness believers passed into eternity, the church began to lose its fervency and became more of an organization than a living organism. After the government of Rome sanctioned Christianity as a religion that was acceptable to the State, the State became more acceptable to the church. Gradually, the separation between the State and the church was lost and what had been the manifestations of power in the Holy Spirit became the manipulations of powerful men who would use their influence to gain wealth and prominence.

As the Emperor Constantine commissioned the building of beautifully decorated cathedrals for Christian worship, the secret gatherings in the homes of the faithful became a thing of the past. And with this change, came a change in the ministry, as the design of these basilicas created a separation between the leaders and the congregation. As the church grew more stratified, the bishops and priest began to take on more power as they were given oversight over territorial "sees" or diocese.

In some cases, bishops became corrupt as they preoccupied themselves with politics and power. This marked the beginning of a greater rift in the ministry, as the church leaders elevated themselves above the people, putting forth the argument that as He had given Peter the Keys to the kingdom, Jesus' intention was to pass that authority down to every bishop who succeeded Peter in the church—particularly at Rome. And the corruption grew greater, as bishops not only took authority over people, but also over other bishops with less territorial responsibility, conferring titles on themselves like Metropolitan, Archbishop or Patriarch.

Historian, Jonathan Hill writes:

> The riches and power that the church acquired practically overnight set uneasily with the poverty of Jesus and the

simplicity of his message, it is said, whilst the association
of bishops with emperors led to complacency, corruption
and a distorted worldview. [5]

Through the ages and dispensations of the church
there have been revivals and restorations, renewals
and reformations, challenges and changes. From the
establishment of the Universal Catholic Church to the
Protestant reformation; from the Methodist/Wesleyan
"second blessing" of sanctification to the Pentecostal
Revivals in Wales and Azusa California, the church
has changed and grown. And perhaps some of the
changes were necessary to minister to the unique
needs of their times.

Still, the questions must be asked: Is the church that
exists today the same church that Jesus instituted—
If not in structure and appearance, then in spirit and
practice? In changing our organizational structures
and adapting our methods, have we drifted away from
the Faith?

I believe the answer can still be found in this
challenge from God's Word;

"Earnestly contend for the faith which was once... "

The wording in this challenge suggests an on-going
struggle, a vigilance and watchfulness "lest we being
led away with the error of the wicked, fall from [our]
own steadfastness" (2 Peter 3:17)

This challenge calls us to re-discover the truth of the gospel as it was originally intended, and to recall and embrace God's agenda in revealing His Christ. The calling to *earnestly contend* challenges us to re-direct our thinking and re-think our direction as we re-examine our motive, our method and our message.

Let's revisit the comments of Matt Casper.

"Plant more churches, help those in need, or make people into millionaires".

After touring churches across the U. S. as well as across the racial and denominational spectrum, Casper was unsure of what the message and the ministry of the church was. In his closing thoughts, he left this sobering question with Pastor Henderson;

"Jim, is this what Jesus told you guys to do?"

Being raised in and around church, and having traveled across the country from convention to convocation, and from festival to fund-raiser, I find myself challenged by that question. That question and the nagging thoughts in my own mind: Do we really have an understanding of God's purpose for the church? Do we have an understanding of the Faith—what its true message is and who that message is intended for? Do we have a real understanding of the power that God has made available to us; and what that power was intended to do?

Using the first century church as a model, perhaps we can re-discover and re-capture The Faith... as it was once.

THE FOUNDATIONS OF OUR FAITH

The Christian faith, simply stated, is faith in the Christ: the belief that God sent a redeemer to reconcile mankind to Himself; that the Christ (Greek translation of the title; "Messiah") was sent as God's *Anointed One*, the spotless sacrifice that would fulfill the law as it had been established in the ancient ordinances.

The first Christians were emphatic on this cornerstone of The Faith; the conviction that the Christ, in fact, had come. They had the advantage, however, of having lived through the events surrounding the ministry of the Messiah. Israel, as a nation, had waited and watched for the fulfillment of the messianic prophecies for over four hundred years. By the time the first church had been established, the rumors and disputes concerning the Christ; His miracles, His crucifixion and resurrection were a matter of everyday discussion, and the Person of Jesus was the subject of debate among religious scholars, scribes and philosophers. To the Christian of the first century, the coming of the Messiah was more than an article of faith, it was a matter of fact.

It is not possible for us to go back in time to experience the events of Jesus' life and ministry; to actually see the miracles at His hand, to sit at His feet and hear the wonder of His wisdom, to be touched and changed by Him, and to know, beyond a shadow of a doubt, that He is the Christ. But, in order to live out The Faith and bear witness to its truth, we must have a secure foundation for our belief.

For many outside The Faith (and sadly, for too many who profess to be in The Faith) Christianity is no more than a choice of religion; a conscious decision to choose the Christian faith over another belief system for our own personal reasons. Perhaps it is because we were taught Christianity as the faith of our parents or because it was the predominant faith of our culture. Maybe it was the only belief we were exposed to, so we chose to follow the Christian Way out of ignorance of another philosophy. Whatever the reason for our belief, skeptics have become convinced that Christianity has no basis in fact. Therefore, it cannot be proved and must be accepted on blind faith... if at all.

But if Christianity is no more than a conscious choice based on emotions or sub-conscious peer pressure, then we worship in vain, a God who cannot hear, who cannot answer and who cannot save.

If we are to contend for this faith, we must be certain, within our own hearts and minds that it is based in fact. And even though we were not there with the first church, I believe that we can confirm our faith in Christ today on these three premises: The authenticity of the Scriptures, the reality of Jesus, and the revelation of the Christ

THE AUTHENTICITY OF THE SCRIPTURES

Over the last several years, intellectuals, critics, and skeptics have sought to compromise or convolute the truth of the Bible; challenging its authenticity by offering alternate gospels or philosophies, or new revelations designed to change the way we view The Faith. The recently discovered Gnostic Gospels, the "Secret Gospel" of Thomas, the so-called gospels of Peter and Judas or the Gospel of Mary Magdalene have all made their debut on the stage of religious discussion and debate, all proclaiming some new discovery that will re-shape the current view of Christianity. In truth, this deception is not a new one, but dates back to the first century A.D. and is addressed by the Apostles in their warnings to the church.

Throughout the New Testament, the warnings against the false prophets of another gospel and another Jesus punctuate the letters of Paul, Peter, John and Jude. Multiple references to this deception can be found in 2 Corinthians 11:13-14, Galatians 1:6-7, Colossians 2:8-19, 1 Timothy 1:3-7, 2 Peter 2:1, Jude 4 and 1 John 4:1.

In Matthew 24 verse 11 and again in verse 24, Jesus himself warns the church that false prophets would rise up and draw away many souls, almost to the point of deceiving those God has chosen.

To the Bible believing Christian, these passages of Scripture should have served as a warning that false teachers and erroneous doctrines would attack the church like a viral infection. Yet, it seems that so many of us know so little about the Bible, how it came to us, and how we can know it's true.

In many of the classes I've conducted, the usual response to my question; "How do you know that the Bible is the Word of God?" has been... By faith.

In an impromptu Bible discussion with a small group of young adults, I was surprised to find how many of them genuinely loved the Lord and believed the gospel, but still had doubts as to whether or not the Bible was absolutely true. I appreciated their honesty, or as they put it—*real talk*—but it brought sharp focus to another reality: many of us (myself included) accepted what we were told about the Bible without ever examining its veracity or truthfulness.

In John 20:29, Jesus admonishes one disciple who challenged the report of His resurrection with these words; "Thomas, because thou hast seen me, thou hast believed: blessed are they that have not seen, and yet have believed."

This statement almost carries the implication that the Word must be taken on blind faith alone. But I would suggest here, that this admonition is more directed at Thomas for doubting, since he had first-hand, eyewitness experience of all that the Lord had done. My reason for this is based in another passage of Scripture found in Acts 17:10 and 11, where the writer makes note of a group of scholars in the city of Berea. These students of Scripture were called more noble than those the disciples had addressed in other cities because, not only did they receive the gospel with readiness of mind, they went further and researched the information to determine if the things that they had been told were true. Imagine the steadfastness of their faith, when they knew in their hearts, as well as in their minds that what they had believed was factual. In that era, there was enough confidence in the original Scriptures that, even though there had been false teachers and false gospels, the genuine seeker could read for themselves to determine truth from error.

Their confidence in the Scripture came from the fact that they knew its origin and its history. They knew how it had been meticulously preserved, and how copies had been made according to strict rules when the original texts had become old and worn. And they knew that their Scriptures not only contained the Word of God, but the history of their people and their identity.

But for our generation—centuries after these documents were recorded (many of which seem to have no relevance to our history or heritage) and now that the gospel and what we have come to know as the New Testament have been added to the books—how can we verify or validate its accuracy, and for that matter, why should we?

Simply stated, if the Bible is not true, then we need to know that so we can discover what is true and follow that truth... or so we can determine that there is no truth or that truth cannot be known (much like the relativistic philosophies of today). But if the Bible is true, it stands to reason that we should search it out; its origin, its history, and its validity, so that—like the Bereans we can stand firm in our faith, assured in our hearts and in our minds that our faith is founded upon fact.

As we begin our search, we want to look at three areas that I believe we can trust to validate our faith in the written Word: history, archeology and prophecy.

HISTORY

The Word of God continually proves to be historically accurate as biblical references to people, places and events are supported by discoveries uncovered by modern day archeologists (we will discuss this shortly). But the authenticity of the Bible is more accurately expressed in its own history and the fact that its revelation was not restricted to any one individual or secret order.

"Knowing this first, that no prophecy of the Scripture is of any private interpretation. For the prophecy came not in old time by the will of man: but holy men of God spake as they were moved by the Holy Ghost"
(2 Peter 1:20-21)

As recorded by Peter, the Scriptures were not the product of the human intellect, but were inspired by Gods Spirit. When we consider this; the Scriptures were not given to one man writing from his own private revelation or imagination, but were recorded by over forty different writers who lived in different areas at different times over a period of fifteen hundred years, and that these writers did not confer with one another and yet they wrote one continuous narrative detailing the history of Gods interaction with and intervention in the affairs of men. Though there were several writers, surely there was only *one* Author who directed their hands.

The ancient record of these writers introduces us to God, His plan and His purpose for our redemption. Put another way—from Genesis to Revelation, the Bible is the written record of God's plan to reconcile mankind back to Himself through Jesus Christ.

The five books of the Law (called the Pentateuch or the Torah) describe Gods initial contact and covenant with man. The historic books from Joshua to Esther explore the story of God's interaction with those He had chosen to manifest His Person and His Power. The books of prophecy, from Isaiah to Malachi unfold Gods plan for our redemption. The Gospel, as recorded by Matthew, Mark, Luke and John reveal the fulfillment of that plan in Jesus the Christ. The Acts of the Apostles and the Letters (Epistles) to the church provide a history of the birth of the church and instructions on Christian conduct in preparation for the completion of God's plan. And lastly, John's Revelation is the prophetic scenario, detailing the conclusion of all the events that culminate in our ultimate salvation and reconciliation to God.

The continuity of this narrative and the unity of thought and purpose through the pen of these writers certainly lend itself to the belief that only the One Spirit could be the author of such an epic work.

In 1Timothy 3:16, Paul writes;

"All Scripture is given by inspiration of God."

Here, he refers to what we have come to know as the Old Testament, or the original Hebrew Bible. In fact, throughout the gospels, Jesus cites the ancient texts using the phrase; "It is written" as a regular part of His message. This reference alone lets us know that He had absolute confidence in the authenticity and accuracy of the Law and the Prophets. But how can we have that kind of confidence in an ancient book that was written centuries before our time?

In Deuteronomy 31:24-28, Moses commissioned the Levites to maintain the Scriptures in a compartment of the Ark of the Covenant, but over time they were neglected and forgotten, only to be re-discovered years later during the reign of King Josiah, as recorded in 2 Kings 22:8. Since there were no methods for preserving written texts in ancient times, there are no remaining manuscripts of the original Scriptures—or of any other ancient texts for that matter. What we do have, however, are the copies that were made over and over until there was a means of preserving them.

Author Josh McDowell notes that the original Hebrew Scriptures were meticulously copied in exacting detail which included specific instructions for the types of animal skins to be used for the scrolls, the size and number of the columns, the type of ink that would be used, the spacing between the words, the lines of print and the number of letters. The scribes who were charged with this responsibility were even required to perform certain rituals before they could write the name of God and were further prohibited from writing anything from memory. The spaces, lines and letters were numbered and counted methodically and if one mistake was found, the entire manuscript would be discarded as faulty and would be destroyed.[6] In actuality, it wasn't the chapters or the verses that were copied, but *every letter and every space.*

In the 1890's over two hundred thousand ancient manuscripts were discovered in a synagogue in Cairo, Egypt, ten thousand of which were biblical. And in 1947, a series of biblical scrolls were discovered in a cave near the Dead Sea. These "Dead Sea Scrolls" were determined to be at least one thousand years older than the earliest copies of the Hebrew Scriptures.

After a comparative study, it was concluded that the scrolls were 95 percent word for word accurate, with the remaining 5 percent error being differences in spelling. The meaning and context of the texts in the Scriptures and the discovered manuscripts were identical, supporting the accuracy of the biblical copies with no changes or differences in context. [7]

The New Testament gospel was transmitted orally, through the preaching and teaching ministries of the Apostles. The actual writings came about as the church requested that a written record be made of the events. Matthew and John, eyewitnesses to the actual events, wrote out their accounts of the ministry of the Messiah. Mark and Luke wrote as the details were shared with them by the Apostles.

To a person outside of The Faith, the methodical way in which the Bible was recorded, and the meticulous way in which it was preserved may still not be sufficient evidence for accepting its validity. But the authenticity of the Bible goes beyond blind faith in the miraculous because the histories, prophecies and the record of the gospel contained in its pages are also supported by archeological discoveries that offer substantial proof of the existence of the people, places and events that the Bible speaks of, many of which, critics said never existed.

ARCHEOLOGY

Archeological digs have verified the existence as well as the destruction of ancient Sodom and Gomorrah in the exact location described in the Bible—complete with the pitch residue from its "fire and brimstone" and the fusing together of the stones that resulted from the intense heat. The discovery of the five porches of the pool at Siloam where Jesus healed the impotent man is among the ten top archeological finds listed in the periodical, "Biblical Archeological Review" [8] Evidence of the destruction of the walls of Jericho and the excavation of the foundations of the Kingdoms of David and Solomon have been tangible discoveries that substantiate the biblical record. [9]

Throughout the late nineteenth and early twentieth centuries, there have been multiple discoveries that have produced irrefutable evidence of the historical accuracy of the biblical account, in fact more than time will allow for this work. For the serious student (and even for the skeptic) I recommend subscribing to the magazine; "Biblical Archeological Review" published by the Biblical Archeological Society, Washington, DC. or visiting their web site at www.biblicalarcheology. org for a wealth of information that supports our faith in the validity of the Bible.

Though the discovery of these ancient kingdoms, temples, ruins and archeological finds prove that the biblical history is accurate, yet they don't prove that the Scripture is inspired by the Spirit of God.

Even though the Bible continually proves its accuracy through comparison of its copies with the texts of the Dead Sea Scrolls and other ancient documents, and though its historical data is supported by the discoveries of archeologists, it is the prophetic writings in its pages that serve to authenticate the Scriptures as inspired or "God-breathed" .

PROPHECY

Prophecy can be called the foretelling of future events or the *forth-telling* of Gods plan and His will for mankind. In an unusual statement (especially for those who don't believe in the accuracy of the Bible) the writers of the ancient Hebrew Scriptures set the standard for its authenticity,

> *"And if thou say in thine heart, How shall we know the word which the Lord hath not spoken? When a prophet speaketh in the name of the Lord, if the thing follow not, nor come to pass, that is the thing which the Lord hath not spoken, but the prophet hath spoken it presumptuously"*
>
> (Deuteronomy 18:20-21)

Here, the Bible is disqualifying itself if its prophecies fail to materialize. But in order to authenticate the prophecies of the Bible, we need to know when they were written and when or if they were fulfilled.

The Hebrew Scriptures or the Old Testament were completed with the books of Malachi and the Chronicles and closed to any new entries after 400 B.C. some four hundred years prior to the time of Jesus. These writings were kept in the Temple at Jerusalem, and preserved in the method we discussed earlier. Because of this process, everything that had been prophesied in its pages had been kept sealed and unchanged for at least four centuries. The prophetic writings of the Scriptures not only foretold the coming of the Messiah (which we will discuss in the next segment) but also forecast the restoration of the nation of Israel through the prophecies of Jeremiah.

There are those who affirm that the Bible makes roughly 2500 prophetic statements, 2000 of which have already been fulfilled to the letter. But I single out the prophecies of Jeremiah as well as the prophetic words of Amos, Isaiah and Zechariah because their fulfillment can be verified through contemporary history.

Around 750 B.C. Amos prophesied the rebuilding of the ruins of Israel (Amos 9:11-12.) After the reign of David, Israel had been conquered and destroyed by the Babylonians, the Assyrians and the Romans and remained in ruins for two thousand years. The re-building and restoration of Israel started as Jews began to return during the early 1900's and is ongoing even as of this writing. This return was prophesied by Isaiah between 701-681 B.C. (Isaiah 43:5-6.) In 1948, Israel was re-established as a sovereign nation, (Jeremiah 31; 38-40) and as recently as 1991, the last of the Jews who had been scattered throughout the world were airlifted from Ethiopia.

In the late 5th century B.C. Zechariah prophesied the return of the Jews to Jerusalem (Zechariah 8:7-8.) This took place in 1967 during the Six Day War, where the Jews regained control of the ancient city. Again, all of these events can be verified through a cursory research of contemporary history.

With the close of the Old Testament in the fourth century before Christ, it is significant that the prophecies concerning the coming of the Messiah had been sealed and kept in the temple at Jerusalem. It is significant, because these Messianic prophecies described—with pinpoint accuracy, the time, the location and the setting that would usher in God's plan for reconciliation. And, according to the Christian faith, these prophecies were fulfilled in Jesus of Nazareth.

THE REALITY OF JESUS

The proof that the Jesus of the Bible actually existed is found, primarily, in the secular or non-Christian histories of the first and second century A.D. We must bear in mind that, during His lifetime, Jesus did not have the same world-wide recognition that He has today. Consequently, the historians of His time paid little attention to the religious leader of an insignificant sect from an insignificant province. Those who did write, however, not only bore witness to His existence, but to the impact of His message and His ministry.

Hebrew historians, critics and even Greek satirists have all confirmed the fact that Jesus was indeed a flesh and blood individual who interacted with actual characters from history. Among those who wrote about Jesus were Roman historian Cornelius Tacitus (A.D. 55) Greek satirist Lucian, and one historian who is frequently noted in the defense of Jesus' existence; Flavius Josephus.

Josephus was a Jewish leader who had been a Pharisee, a captive prisoner after the fall of Jerusalem and eventually, a Roman citizen. His works; *The Antiquities of the Jews,* which catalogues the history of the Jews from the records of Moses through the reign of Alexander; and *The Wars of the Jews*, which details the insurrection of the Jews against Rome and the subsequent destruction of Jerusalem provide an extensive and in depth look at the history of the Bible from a secular point of view.

For Christians, the most noteworthy passages of Josephus' works are those that speak directly of Jesus. In Antiquities 18.3.3 Josephus writes;

> Now, about this time Jesus, a wise man, if it be lawful to call him a man, for he was a doer of wonderful works- a teacher of such men as receive the truth with pleasure. He drew over to him both many of the Jews and many of the Gentiles.[10]

In 116 A.D. Cornelius Tacitus confirms the existence of Jesus, His followers and the truth of His crucifixion as he addresses the burning of Rome, which had been attributed to the Emperor Nero;

"Therefore, to scotch this rumour, Nero substituted as culprits, and punished with the utmost refinements of cruelty, a class of men, loathed for their vices, whom the crowd styled Christians. Christus, the founder of the name, had undergone the death penalty in the reign of Tiberius, by sentence of the procurator Pontius Pilatus."

And in 170 A.D. Lucian the Satirist wrote;

> "The Christians, you know, worship a man to this day- the distinguished personage who introduced their novel

rites, and was crucified in that account ... you see, these misguided creatures start with the general conviction that they are immortal for all time, which explains the contempt of death and voluntary self-devotion which are so common among them; and then it was impressed on them by their original lawgiver that they are all brothers, from the moment they are converted, and deny the gods of Greece, and worship the crucified sage, and live after his laws."[11]

In these works, Josephus verifies the historical existence of Jesus, Tacitus supports the fact that Jesus was crucified by Pontius Pilate, and (quite unintentionally) Lucian substantiates the biblical record that Jesus was worshipped as the Son of God. The list of Christian historians who wrote of Jesus' ministry and of the experiences of the first century church is quite extensive and can be found in the work *A Dictionary of Early Christian Beliefs* By David W. Bercot.

Among the archeological discoveries that substantiate the biblical account of Jesus' life are the discovery in 1961 of an inscription from Pontius Pilate "Prefect of Judea" and the excavation of the small town of Nazareth in 1962. Both of these support the historicity of the biblical events in proving that the people and the places spoken of in the Bible actually existed.

Again, recall that the Old Testament Scriptures had been sealed in the Temple at Jerusalem for at least four hundred years, prior to the life of Jesus (450-400 BC) So, the prophetic writings concerning the Messiah could not have been altered—at least not without a conspiracy that would include the cooperation of the Jewish Priests and Scribes; a complete compromise and controverting of the Talmud which secured the purity and accuracy of the Hebrew texts; and an investigator who could track and catalogue every event in the life of Jesus and then insert those events in the prophetic texts in the style and language of each prophet. The likelihood of this having happened is implausible if not altogether impossible. This *implausible alternative* notwithstanding, the Hebrew Scriptures spoke of the coming of the Messiah who would reconcile man to God.

In Isaiah 7:14, the prophet recorded these words, "Therefore the Lord Himself will give you a sign: Behold the virgin shall conceive and bear a Son, and shall call His name Immanuel." Micah writes, "But thou, Bethlehem Ephratah, though thou be little among the thousands of Judah, yet out of thee shall he come forth unto me that is to be ruler in Israel; whose goings forth have been from old, from everlasting." (Micah 5:2)

In Zechariah 9:9, the prophet foretells the arrival of the Messiah on a colt, "Rejoice greatly, O daughter of Zion; shout, O daughter of Jerusalem: behold thy King cometh unto thee: he is just, and having salvation; lowly, and riding upon an ass, and upon a colt the foal of an ass." And, again, Isaiah the prophet gives detail to the betrayal, rejection, scourging and death that would be endured by the Messiah. (Isaiah 53)

According to the gospel, and the historic narratives of secular writers; these prophecies were fulfilled, to the letter, in Jesus of Nazareth.

Just as it is with the authenticity of the Scriptures, the life and the ministry as well as the crucifixion and the worship of Jesus are all validated by history, archeology and by the prophetic record. And through all of this information, though we may gain arguing points for biblical accuracy and for the existence of the historical Jesus, there is one thing more that is needed to move us from an intellectual understanding of the facts to an unshakable and undeniable faith.

THE REVELATION OF THE CHRIST

In the passage of Scripture found in Matthew 16:13-17, Jesus challenges the disciples understanding of His Person with the question,

"Whom do men say that I the Son of man am?"

After some random answers that reflected the popular views Jesus asked, "But whom say ye that I am?" The answer to this question is the single most important statement in the Christian faith, because its answer cannot be determined by historical facts, archeological discoveries or by verifying ancient texts. This answer only comes by the revelatory Grace of God. I don't mean this to sound mystical as if this revelation is available only to a certain sect or privileged few, but that the *realization* of this truth is an act of God's revelatory Grace.

Peter answered Jesus, "Thou art the Christ, the Son of the living God." This answer was more profound than all the speculations that had been offered from the popular opinions, because while the response came through Peter, it was not a product of his intellect.

"And Jesus answered and said unto him, Blessed art thou, Simon Barjona; for flesh and blood hath not revealed it unto thee, but my Father which is in heaven."

(Matthew 16:17)

This revelation is the foundation upon which the church is built and it is on the "rock" of this truth that our salvation is based.

Paul writes;

"... if thou shalt confess with thy mouth the Lord Jesus, and shalt believe in thine heart that God hath raised him from the dead, thou shalt be saved. For with the heart man believeth unto righteousness; and with the mouth confession is made unto salvation."

(Romans 10:9)

Again in 1 Corinthians 12:3 he writes;

"Wherefore I give you to understand, that no man speaking by the Spirit of God calleth Jesus accursed: and no man can say that Jesus is the Lord, but by the Holy Ghost."

What separated the first century church from the multitude of other religious sects of that era? What motivated them to bear witness to the truth of the gospel and what made them unashamed to be numbered among the Christians even at the risk of imprisonment or death? I believe it was a conviction based on *first-hand* experience; the personal revelation of Jesus the Christ.

After the first generation eyewitnesses who walked and talked with Jesus, it was those to whom He revealed Himself by the Holy Spirit who "turned the world upside down" by bearing witness to the Lordship of Jesus. The writer of the Acts of the Apostles recorded these words spoken by Jesus:

"But ye shall receive power, after that the Holy Ghost is come upon you: and ye shall be witnesses unto me both in Jerusalem, and in all Judea, and in Samaria, and unto the uttermost part of the earth."

(Acts 1:8)

And here, I'm not in reference to an ecstatic experience or emotional expression, but a genuine revelation by the indwelling presence of God's Spirit that brings the reality of salvation into sharp focus, moving the believer from an intellectual agreement with the facts to an empowered eyewitness *know-so* relationship with a Risen Savior.

It is this indwelling Spirit of God that convinces us of the reality of God in Christ and of Christ in us as His Spirit bears witness within our spirits that *Jesus is Lord.* It is this experience that empowered, emboldened and motivated the first century church. And it is only this experience that will empower, embolden and motivate us today for the enormous task of reaching the cities for Jesus.

This is The Faith which was once, and The Faith we must contend for; faith in the Living God who can be known, as the early believers knew Him; faith that confirms within our spirits the Lordship of Jesus the Christ; and faith that motivates us to unashamedly bear witness to the truth of the gospel. We can and must be empowered, emboldened and motivated to stand for the Faith, not just on Sunday in the safety of our sanctuaries, but daily and in every situation, ready to affirm its truth.

"...and be ready always to give an answer to every man that asketh you a reason of the hope that is in you..."

(1 Peter 3:15)

CHAPTER FIVE

A TIME TO RUN

"And Moses said unto Aaron, Take a censer, and put fire therein from off the altar, and put on incense, and go quickly unto the congregation, and make an atonement for them: for there is wrath gone out from the Lord; the plague is begun"

(Numbers 16:46).

I watched an extremely disturbing documentary about the Los Angeles gang scene, as told by the gang members themselves in their own words and from their point of view. The interviews and stories covered young men whose lives had been shaped by the harsh reality of gangs, drugs, and poverty—a few of them, murdered before the filming could be completed. It wasn't as much the violent culture of the streets that bothered me as it was the acceptance of violence as a way of life, the casual attitudes about the value they placed on the lives of others—and for that matter—their own lives, and their resolution to this lifestyle as they frequently made the comment, "This is all we know."

Throughout the documentary, although there were expressions of sadness and remorse as they lost friends and relatives through gang violence, never once did any one of them come to the realization that their situation could change, or that it was within their power to change it. It was as if they had accepted and embraced the fact of their own destruction—unalterable, unavoidable and inescapable.

As I watched, my heart was grieved because I felt my efforts to reach them were almost futile. The destruction of an entire generation seemed imminent and immediate, and for the moment, I felt powerless to do anything about it. Then, the Word of God spoke to me directly, as my pastor preached the solution.

The sixteenth chapter of the book of Numbers recounts a series of incidents that resulted in a crisis of destruction that threatened to destroy an entire generation. By their own choices, this generation willfully placed themselves in the direct path of God's wrath.

From the priestly tribe of Levi; Korah, Dathan and Abiram had been selected to serve, offering sacrifices and maintaining the sacred articles of worship. These duties placed them in a position of great prestige and honor, but in their arrogance they presumed upon themselves to take on the mantle of leadership and organized a group of leaders in opposition to Moses.

These priests presented a popular gospel, preaching those things that the people wanted to hear; a life of ease and prosperity under Egyptian rule, in contrast to the challenge, uncertainty and responsibility that comes with freedom. And to people who have endured the hardships of life, returning to bondage might certainly appear to be easier. A return to bondage would eliminate the stress and responsibility of making their own decisions. Allowing someone (or something) to control their destiny, would relieve them of the perceived stress of having to be obedient to God—especially when that obedience would take them out of their comfort zone—and a return to slavery would provide the security of home in contrast to the challenge of following God when all they could see in front of them was wilderness.

In a miraculous display, at the word of Moses, God caused the ground to open and "swallow up" the rebellious priests, their tents, their families and everything that pertained to them. But rather than recognize and reverence the authority of God, the people willfully chose to follow their self-styled leaders even though they had just witnessed the wrath of God against them. As a result of their own choices ,they faced the same destruction as those they chose to follow.

As God revealed His anger and His plan, Moses' first response was one of concern for his people. In spite of the fact that they had accused him of misleading them into an uncertain wilderness; in spite of the fact that they had disobeyed God and disrespected His leadership; in spite of their rebellion Moses' first thoughts were for their salvation. Even as God spoke, Moses had enough insight to understand the immediacy of the moment; there would be no forestalling of judgment and no deferment of the destruction.

Judgment was imminent, and the need to act was immediate. There would be no time to consult with political leaders or influential people, no time to organize a march to draw attention to the problem, and no time to raise money to support his ministry. Moses had to act, and *act quickly* because an entire generation was at risk and the destruction had already begun.

It was because Moses had a relationship with the Lord, that he knew precisely what to do... and how to do it. His instructions to the priest, "Take a censer, and put fire therein from off the altar, and put on incense, and go quickly unto the congregation, and make an atonement for them."

EMPOWER EQUIP ENGAGE

Moses' first order of business was to empower the priest to minister outside of the sanctuary. He recognized that while the church held the solution to the problem, that solution would only be effective at the place of the need... the center of the crisis. Moses released Aaron from his responsibilities in the sanctuary and authorized him to take ministry outside and into the midst of the very people who had rejected him and who had rejected God. In doing this, Moses set a significant precedent: there needs to be a relationship between the priesthood and the neighborhood.

There needs to be a relationship between the priesthood and the neighborhood.

Then Moses equipped the priest with the solution to the problem; the censer, fire from the altar, and incense. The censer was the peculiar vessel that had been sanctified—cleansed and set apart to be used in the sacrifice that would bring about the atonement between God and the people. This would be the *vehicle* to deliver the solution. The censer would then be filled with coals of fire from the altar. This fire represented the Spirit of God and His power to ignite and illuminate everything that He touches. And upon the burning coals, Aaron was to place the aromatic incense that represented the prayers of the faithful. The sanctified vessel, the fire of God's Spirit, the power of prayer; these elements were all that were needed to save the people.

Today, in a very real sense, we are called to become the censers; the vessels that God would use as the vehicle to deliver the message of salvation. The sanctification of our vessels does not refer to a condescending holier-than-thou display of self-righteousness, but to the living out of our faith in the practical day-to-day applications that exemplify righteousness in the way we conduct ourselves, in the way we treat one another and in the image that we present to those outside The Faith.

Paul wrote to the church at Corinth; "Ye are our epistle written in our hearts, known and read of men" (2 Cor 3:2). In everyday language, what Paul was saying to the church is that *we* are the book that men read. Many people will never read the Bible, but they will *read* the Christian who professes to live by it. Even the most callous skeptic cannot argue with the example of a life that has been transformed by an encounter with Jesus.

Regrettably, this generation has seen an unprecedented number of scandals, as lawsuits against faith-leaders for fiscal malfeasance and sexual impropriety have been made public through the news media as well as the internet. And, in turn, this has had a devastating effect on the credibility of the Christian witness and of our faith.

When we understand that the world judges our faith—not based on what we say, but what we do—we will understand the need to live out the principles of those things we say we believe.

As God's sanctified vessels, we must be illuminated by the fire of God's Holy Spirit. The reference to God's indwelling Spirit, according to Acts 1:8, directs us to His purpose; to empower the believer to be an effective witness. Not for the purpose of an ecstatic experience (although, being in the express presence of God may bring about that very thing). God's indwelling Spirit empowers us to be effective in sharing the message of His reality and of His power to transform lives. It is this indwelling that moves the believer from an intellectual agreement with the things we've read or have been taught to an experiential awareness of the reality of God in Christ and of Christ in us—the hope of Glory and the message of salvation. This is empowerment.

This is *Power with a Purpose*; God's Spirit alive in us bearing witness to the truth of His Word.

Our sanctified vessels, illuminated and empowered by the fire of God's Spirit must then be further empowered by fervent prayer. I cannot overstate the importance of establishing and maintaining an active and consistent prayer-life. Ephesians 6:12 states "We wrestle not against flesh and blood, but against principalities, against powers, against the rulers of the darkness of this world, against spiritual wickedness in high places"

Our struggle is not one of flesh and blood, but of spirit. We are not at war with the sinner, but with the spirit that drives and dominates his life. Prayer is not only our weapon, but our preparation as we take the battle into the realm of the spiritual.

Moses final instruction to Aaron was to move with haste, take the same authority that he exercised in the church and put it to work at the place of the need. What Aaron took with him was the power to make atonement for the sins of the people; to reconcile or bring them back into a right relationship with God.

God's intention in sending us out of the sanctuary can be summed up in this passage of Scripture;

"And all things are of God, who hath reconciled us to himself by Jesus Christ, and hath given to us the ministry of

reconciliation; to with, that God was in Christ, reconciling the world unto himself, not imputing their trespasses unto them; and hath committed unto us the word of reconciliation. Now then we are ambassadors for Christ, as though God did beseech you by us: we pray you in Christ's stead, be ye reconciled to God."

(2 Corinthians 5:18-20)

Into the midst of the destruction, into the midst of the plague, even into the midst of death, Moses sent the holy priest, the sanctified vessel, the fire of God's Spirit, and the power of prayer. And in this same fashion, God has commissioned us as His priests, His vessels, and yes... His ambassadors.

WHAT ARE YOU PREPARED TO DO?

When I look at the devastation of an entire generation of young men and young women from the inner cities and barrios of our country, I realize that this problem is not a distant threat or a deferred judgment but that the destruction of a generation of African American and Latino youth is a pressing and present reality. And no, I'm not being fatalistic or pessimistic; I am aware that there are those who have escaped the plague of gangs, violence, drugs, and imprisonment—but the vast numbers of those who have not should ring like an alarm in our minds. As drive-by shootings and drug sales proliferate in our communities; as gang members commit acts of violence on our church parking lots and inside our sanctuaries; and as prisons are overcrowded with our young where they are recruited and trained to become better criminals we have to recognize that the destruction has already begun.

When I think of the urgency to act, two quotes come to mind. The first from eighteenth century statesman and philosopher, Edmund Burke; "The only thing necessary for the triumph of evil is for good men to do nothing." The second quote comes from the motion picture *The Untouchables*.

In a scene between Kevin Costner as Elliott Ness and Sean Connery as Officer Jim Malone, Connery's character utters his dying last words "What are you prepared to do?"

Both of these quotes serve as motivators for me. The first because it challenges me from the standpoint of my faith. It stands to reason that if a person who is merely a *good man* is called to take a stand against the challenge of that which is evil, how much more should the Christian who has been empowered by God's Word and his Spirit?

Just as Aaron was empowered and released to take the vessels out of the temple and into the midst of a dying people, our ministers and ministries must be empowered equipped and engaged to minister to a generation that seems destined to destruction. The priests, empowered to move out among a people who are still dying; the vessels, filled with the fire of God's Holy Spirit and the power of fervent prayer; these are still the most essential elements needed to save the people. Yet, we huddle inside of our churches—our doors are gated and our windows barred—praying for God to do *something*, when he has empowered us precisely for that purpose.

It would be foolish to suggest that these precautions are not without their causes. In recent years, the physical church has become the scene of gang shootings, a target for thieves and vandals and even a stage for vicious attacks by angry lovers over suspicions of unfaithfulness.

I believe that much of this is the direct result of the disconnect between the church and the community that it has been charged to serve. Paraphrasing Dr. Gregory Alex of Seattle Washington's Matt Talbot Center; the people of the community can't see a relationship between the church and their reality. Or worse—they see the church as a siphon, draining their resources without making any contribution. And many of our troubled young people can't seem to find any connection to the church at all.

I read an interesting article, a few years ago by a young writer from the violent streets of one our major cities. The writer lamented the death of a friend whose life had been cut short by gun violence. What captured my attention wasn't the fact that the writer mourned the passing of another child in the city, but the idea that perhaps the persons' life might have been spared had the local church been available and open to him.

In an article for YO! Youth Outreach, Swan Gantt writes;

> I've noticed that many churches put bars on the windows and lock their gates. Maybe church folks are scared of young folks. Sometimes we don't know how to act: cussin' in the church and disrespecting parents and elders. It's like the church is a sanctuary for all the parents, a place they can go to be away from us. That needs to change.[1]

That needs to change.

In my experience, too many of our churches are gated and barred. We have gated ourselves in, and barred out those who don't fit in our church culture; those who need our help and influence the most.

I took part in a city-wide Cease Fire march, sponsored by a small group of churches. The march, though organized by a Christian group, was set up as an ecumenical effort in order to accommodate the participation of those non-Christian organizations that might be willing to help.

Because the group was ecumenical in nature, we were instructed not to share the Faith, pray with or proselytize any of the people we might encounter (I'll speak to that, later). My initial assumption was that the intent of this group was to quell the violence by the sheer presence of our number. The sound of gunfire exchange a short distance away convinced me that, like many of our secular efforts, we only succeeded in moving the problem to another area rather than solving it.

The group followed a prescribed plan of action as we walked the dark streets from 7 until 9 p.m... but I had another objective in mind. Like Nehemiah, my plan was to spy out the city by night, to get a first-person view of the problems that challenge the city. What I saw disturbed me more deeply than the young man begging for hand-outs or the woman leaning against the liquor store wall trying to scrounge up enough change to buy her next bottle.

I saw churches on practically every corner, and several on the main street—most in view and in walking distance of one another. And with the exception of one small store-front church, they were all closed! Gated, shut, windows barred, lights off, not open for business on Friday night... CLOSED!

There was not a prayer or a sermon to be heard, almost as if the church were sending the message, "We've surrendered the night to Satan."

I remembered the old fashioned Friday night prayer and revival services that poor souls like me would stagger into—drunk or high, but drawn in by the power of prayer, the call of the preacher or even the sound of the tambourine. I was disturbed because, much like Swann Gantt, I knew that people who were hurting might have been helped had the church doors been opened.

As we sit in the safety of our sanctuaries, the communities that God has entrusted to us fall into ruin. While we worship in our comfortable pews, our neighborhoods languish. And while we secure the blessings of the Lord for ourselves and our children, the children in our communities are literally dying on the sidewalks just outside our doors. In a very real sense because of our actions (or our failure to act) we are causing Edmund Burke's words to become a self-fulfilling prophecy.

"The only thing necessary for the triumph of evil is for good men to do nothing."

When I consider preparedness, especially in the context of the second quote, it speaks more to me of commitment than of preparation. What are we *committed* to do? What are we willing to commit—what are we willing to *put on the line*—in order to reach a generation that has chosen a path that will lead to their destruction? What are we *prepared* to do?

As we sat in the church, making our final preparation for the Cease-Fire march, we were counseled not to offer prayer and not to offer salvation to those people we might encounter, since this was an ecumenical effort.

In the years that I have attended seminars, symposiums and civic meetings that center their focus on addressing the problems that plague urban America, never once have I heard anyone from any other faith group fail to acknowledge or honor their belief system. Their profession of faith (whether Muslim, Buddhist or Atheist) might find its way into their opening statement or into the body of their remarks, but there would be no question as to what they believed or the impact that they felt their beliefs would have on the subject at hand.

I bristled at the thought of having a Christian leader charge those Christians in attendance *not* to share the message of hope with people who appeared to have lost all hope. And in barring us from sharing the gospel, the sponsoring church actually rendered us powerless to introduce the very help that the people needed—the power of the gospel to change lives.

All too often, we as Christians are so inclined to avoid confrontation with people of other faiths that we, in effect, *deny our own.* We avoid conflict in the name of being peacemakers, but the need for peacemakers is at the center of the conflict... and that is where we are charged to go.

So, the question remains; *what are we prepared to do?*

Are we prepared to take a stand for Jesus in the face of those who have willfully determined to reject Him? Are we prepared to defend the Faith where others have embraced the message of inclusivity—that all religions lead to God?

Are we prepared to take our faith out of the sanctuary and into the midst of the conflict and the crisis? Are we prepared to move outside of our *comfort zones* and into the communities that God has charged us to reach? Are we prepared to give an answer to everyone that asks; a reason of the hope that is in us?

What are we prepared to do?

"And Aaron took as Moses commanded, and ran into the midst of the congregation ... And he stood between the dead and the living: and the plague was stayed"

(Numbers 47-48).

Aaron ran.

This is the time to run. Just as Aaron ran with the censer, the fire and the incense, we must run with our sanctified vessels— indwelt and empowered with the fire from the altar and strengthened by the power of prayer.

Run.

This is the time to release God's Priesthood from the comfort-zone of our sanctuaries and empower them to move into the heart of the conflict.

Run!

This is the not the time to avoid confrontation. This is the time to stand between the dead and the living to declare the atoning Word of reconciliation.

RUN!

There is not time for another march; or another meeting with the City Council; there is no time to solicit support from local politicians or influential people. This is the time for the priesthood to move out into the neighborhood, take our position in the community, and reach out to a dying generation.

This is the Time to Run!

The immediacy and the magnitude of the problem—the availability of highly addictive drugs and high-tech weapons; the devaluing of human life and the disproportionate arrests and incarceration of our youth; dwindling support for educational and social reform and the loss of hope among those who have been disenfranchised make our problems appear to be beyond our ability to solve. And the easiest thing to do would be to retreat into the safety of our gated churches, preach to the choir, collect an offering and go back home to the suburbs. The truth is, for any one individual or one church, one government agency or one civic organization, our problems are just that... beyond our ability.

In researching the data for this work—and to better inform my own ministry—I have discovered that (even though it may not have been deliberate) the forces that have brought about this destruction were very coordinated in their efforts—those who provided the drugs and the guns and ensured that they remained largely in the inner cities and those who profit from the sales; those whose political careers benefit from the fear of crime; and those private industries who have built their economy on bigger and better jails.

Almost as if by design, these forces—from the cocaine cartels to the street-corner hustler; from the munitions manufacturer to the prisons for profit; and from the pimp to the politician—have all come together despite their differences to bring about this crisis and they have all benefitted from it. And, as much as I hate to admit it, through their choices, this generation has cooperated with them to their own destruction.

When we recognize that these problems are not isolated incidents, but the result of a sophisticated network of events and groups, we should understand that the solution must also come from an equally sophisticated network, organized and orchestrated to address the issues... and this is where I hold out hope.

The battle for the soul of this generation (and that's precisely what I believe this to be) goes beyond our political, denominational, racial, and cultural differences and calls for us to rise above those differences to become a sophisticated network of ministries, enlisting and engaging the strengths and the skills, the experience and the expertise of every priest.

I hold out hope because a movement has started. Quietly, without fanfare, and (in some cases) without the structure—or the stricture—of the organized church, priests are beginning to leave the safety of the sanctuaries and go out into the streets and meet the people at the point of their needs. Ministers and ministries are beginning to take their sanctified vessels, ignited by the fire of God's Holy Spirit and are taking a stand between the dead and the living.

On the following pages, I've invited a few of these priests to share their experiences, their testimonies, their passions, and their solutions as they do their part to stay the plague. These are God's sanctified vessels, gone out into the midst of the conflict to declare the message of reconciliation. I pray that their ministries, their message and their courage will inspire you to take your priesthood into the neighborhood.

The destruction has already begun.

This is a time to run.

PART 2

THE
CALLING

CHAPTER SIX

EVANGELIZING AN EMERGING CULTURE

Scott A. Bradley

G enerations are associated with and even defined by their signature which often leaves an imprint or contribution to the overall society. These generations contribute to the lingo, arts and attitudes that in some cases have even changed the culture itself. The American Culture has greatly changed within the past 25 years. The attitudes of morality are slowly fading from the society that we are living in as biblical standards are being forsaken for "Modern Thought". One of the reasons has to do with the current generation's rebellion of the 70's. During this era the youth had rebelled against the establishment, coining phrases like, "Do your thing" "If it feels good, do it" "Let it all hang out!"

They took on such monikers as "Hippies, Beatniks, and Flower Children" They rebelled against the "Establishment" particularly because of the Viet Nam War that was raging at the time and felt that the direction being taken by the country was leading them to destruction. Although history has proven that America's involvement in Viet Nam was a mistake, it all was a contributing factor to a changing of tactics in the American Culture.

There was a term used to describe the rebellion called "The Generation Gap" This in short meant that the younger generation was not only rejecting the wisdom of the previous, but looking at them as enemies of the advancement of the culture. It was also defined by "free love", free-sex" with less emphasis of the sacred institute of marriage along with the elimination of what otherwise was shameful behavior. However, it was just a matter of time until that generation of Hippies, Beatniks, and Flower Children grew up and became a part of the current society. The phrases of the 70's became the standard of the current generation. Hence, the attitude of the culture changed reflecting the rebellion of the people. "If it feels good, do it, "Let it all hang out" and "Do your thing!" is no longer what they said in the 70's, but they do in the present. It is therefore easier for the culture to accept things such as pre-marital sex, abortion, homosexuality, and common-law marriages.

Because of this there are great challenges to 21st century ministry. It appears that shame is non-existent. Whereas at one time it was taboo to live in Common-Law marriage, or for a young lady to become pregnant out of wedlock, the attitude of the culture now excepts this is normal and even encourages it. Homosexuality, when at one time was looked down upon now has the endorsement from the highest office in the country— the President of the United States. And now, there are even openly Gay churches.

Political Correctness is now more important to the culture than the Bible and Christian principles. In fact, Christianity in the minds of many is outdated and much of the upcoming generations are exploring new religions and new philosophies. So the challenges are greater because the American Culture has changed.

Therefore one of the first things that one must understand in Christian ministry is that the 21st century American Culture is offended by traditional Christian principles and the minister must be aware now more than ever that his message may not be readily accepted. He may face challenges from other religions, particularly with the rise of Islam.

The preaching of the Gospel must be done with conviction, influenced by the Holy Spirit of God, with an uncompromising fervor. God's Word is right. There is no other alternative. When Jesus said, "I am the way, the truth, and the life; no man cometh to the Father, but by me" (St. John 14:6) the 21st century American Culture would tag this Politically incorrect. All major religions are challenged. If Jesus said He is the only way, then Buddha. Mohammed and all others are false teachers with a false hope. Yet the boldness and directness of this statement clearly shows that He alone is the only way to heaven and that all other ways, no matter how sincere or popular among the mass are in error. He is not showing the way, He is the way. He is not just telling the truth, He is incarnated. He is not just giving life. Life is non-existent except in Him.

THE EVOLUTION OF BLACK CULTURE

Cultures evolve. An example of this change is the Civil Rights Movement of the 50's & 60's. Whereas at one time African American citizen were considered 2nd class and discriminated against without reservation, even backed by laws justifying racism, the movement brought awareness to rights that were afforded to every citizen of the United States, regardless of race, creed or color, and finally made America live up to its own constitution. The movement for the most part changed the culture.

It is also evident in the Civil Rights movement, as the 70's saw a change of a tactics among the younger generation when revolutionaries began to take the movement to a more confrontational and radical way; using a more militant style and coining the phrase "Black Power". The Southern Christian Leadership Conference (SCLC) lead by Christian Ministers like Dr. Martin Luther King Jr. was non-violent; the Black Panthers, lead by such revolutionaries as Stokely Carmichael, were confrontational and militant. Although the radical movement was short-lived, it was still a contributing factor in shaping the attitudes of the current American politics. The combined movements brought a change of thinking in the American psyche which eventually allowed America to elect her first Black President, an idea unheard of just a few generations before.

However, one of the misfortunes within the African-American community is the lack of connection that brings us all in common. Whereas the other ethnic groups can trace back to a basic ancestry of origin;

a homeland as it were, the Black man in American cannot really connect to a culture abroad or a country, but often tries to make a generic connection to the African continent which consists of over 50 countries across a vast land and over 1000 tribes and dialects. The reality is that the African American culture is found more in the Southern part of the Unites States and the influence from various African countries rather one particular African country itself. Black Folks can better ancestrally connect to Mississippi, Alabama, Georgia and Florida than directly to Africa.

Another unfortunate matter within the African-American community is the willingness to forget, disregard or even ignore the past. Many Black families that came from the South to the North during the migrations of the early 20th centuries often did so with bitter memories that they wanted to soon forget. Stories that could have been told and should have been told were not told because the recollections of such stories brought memories and pain, sorrow, bitterness and even fear. Many African Americans took such stories to their graves. No story can better be told than that of the eyewitness. These misfortunes, though not unique among the various cultures are certainly prevalent within the African American culture, and ignorance of the past is far more widespread as we have often made the mistake of letting others tell us our own story.

Forgetting can prove to be more detrimental to the upcoming generations because the victimization of the previous generations can easily be repeated in the present. The Jews will never forget the atrocities of the holocaust during WW II and keep reminders of it among themselves, teaching them to the generations to come. Every Jew is aware that 6 million of their ancestors lost their lives to Hitler and the German Nazi's "Final Solution" Not only will they not forget, they will not let the rest of the world forget.

However, how not many African Americans, or for that fact, anybody else in the world is aware that there was a African holocaust that resulted in the death of an estimated 10 million during the middle passage of the slave trade in the 18th century?

Therefore attitudes are not only created by what we have learned, but by what we have also failed to learn or forgotten from the past. The true saying, "If you don't know where you've been, you won't know where you are going", is obvious within the African American community.

THE CULTURE WITHIN THE CULTURE

Within the African American community the culture of music has evolved from the Spirituals, to Blues: from Jazz to Rhythm & Blues (R&B), to Hip Hop and Rap. The evolution of the cultures also speaks to as well as of the culture. Music has often reflected the message of its generation. The Negro Spirituals were messages of hope often birthed and sang in the slave fields during the horrific times of American slavery when African Americans labored under the brutal task with an apparent hopeless future.

One should note that even within music there is a parallel of the styles in the Spirituals and the contemporaries. As the style of the spirituals changed, so also changed the styles of the contemporaries. The Spirituals spoke a message of hope in hard times, the Blues spoke of hard times usually out of hopeless despair of great loss. Both styles still told a story. As time progressed the music became more upbeat and the Jazz era was introduced. Music in the African American community, with new instrumental arrangement, brought new dance with the message. People began to swing. Much of the music of the era was not necessarily because the people were happy, but it helped them to forget.

When one makes a comparison to the current styles when paralleled, the younger generation has combined the poetic style of story-telling with rapid, rhythmic lyrics called rap. The gangsters tell of the streets and the lifestyles of the "gangtsa" complete with the street language, laced with profanity and derogatory names for women. The less profane tell stories nonetheless of experiences, hopes, and love. Gospel Rap uses the same rapid style to deliver its message. However the message, similar to the old Negro Spirituals includes one of hope for the return of the Lord and the joy of serving him. Gansta rap gives no hope or solution, only an abstract telling of the situation as told by its victims. "This is the reality of the streets", are the justifications for the guttural rhetoric of the gangsta's. However it should be understood that the "rap" style is the signature of the generation, whether, gansta, poetic, or gospel.

It is impossible to say that America has only one culture. After all, American prides herself in being called the Great Melting Pot, a variance and combining all cultures from around the world. Some have evolved, assimilated, and are shared among each other.

It should also be understood that the entire African American community cannot be defined by one culture as the influences vary from different neighborhoods, religious upbringings and class status. This type of influence is common among all ethnic groups in American. All Blacks do not think and act the same, any more than the Italian, Irish, Polish, Jews or any other ethnic groups. Even the cultures among the Native American tribes vary and yet they are still apart of the American Culture. After all they preceded all others in this land.

It is the youth that generally change the culture because of their exposure and openness to those that they become exposed to. As stated earlier, the Civil Rights movement began to see a shift when the young revolutionaries used more radical tactics in attempt to bring change to the American society. Affective ministry takes place when the ministers, whether missionaries, evangelist, or street preachers understands the culture of the one they are ministering to and not arrogantly force their own culture upon another in the name of religion. The minister must understand the difference between preaching the gospel to convert the heart and not necessarily the environment. If environmental change is necessary, it will only take place with a change of heart, attitude and mind. The preaching of the gospel does this.

This is one of the reasons that even to this day the Native Americans still have trouble with American culture because of the way it was forced upon them. The tactics of the American Missionaries, when preaching to the Native American's general was done out of disrespect and arrogance as it was already in the minds of these Missionaries that the Indian tribes were filled with paganism combined with stupidity. In the 1870's Missionaries sent to share the Gospel with the Nes Perce Indians found no success after 10 years of preaching and living among, not winning one convert. One Missionary declared that they were all stupid. However, what is obvious is that if you live among a people for 10 years and cannot persuade one to accept the Good News of the Gospel it is certainly not the fault of the people, but the presenter. One of the arrogances of many of the missionaries was the idea of converting people into their own culture and having no respect or regard for culture of the people they are ministering to. In the case of these Missionaries there mission was not to win the Nes Perce to Christ as much as making them accept white culture and forsake their own, which had great ancestral values and traditions that the white man just didn't understand.

What should also be understood is that everyone does not have a ministry for every type of people. Ministries are affective when its participants understand those that they are ministering to. For example, if one has never been in jail or imprisoned they may not necessarily understand the mind-set of inmates trying to survive in the hostile environment of prison. I am reminded of the young man I knew who took it upon himself to explain to a group of women how to have a baby. He may have watched his wife give birth process but could not speak other than what he observed. Needless to say when those women, who were highly offended at his advice, got through verbally chewing him up and spitting him out...

People want to relate to the person who is ministering to them. They are more likely to open up and trust someone whom they feel has been where they are. This is why people whom the Lord has delivered from a certain environment go right back to it to minister, i.e. former prisoners ministering in the prisons.

THE MINISTRY OF JESUS

When one looks at the Ministry of Jesus it is clear that He knew the affective way of ministering to the people was to speak to them where they were. I am reminded of a religious forum I was in a number of years ago. One of the speakers was given the platform and proceeded to speak about 45 minutes on a subject that I don't remember. The one thing I do remember about his presentation was that it was extremely boring and did not hold my attention longer than 3 minutes. Afterwards I was in the office with the pastor and a few of the other ministers.

"How was the presentation?" He asked. "Boring!" was the overwhelming response. One minister even said, "He spoke too much Greek and Hebrew for me"

The Pastor responded by saying something that to this day has often stills stays in my mind. "People who are trying to impress everyone with how much they know usually only impress themselves"

Jesus never tried to impress people with what He knew. After all, He knew everything. He ministered to the people where they were. He told stories that related to their everyday lives. In order to effectively minister to the culture one must first understand the culture. One must also understand that to talk down to something that you don't understand makes one look arrogant to the ones he is attempting to minister to.

Going back to the words of the Pastor who made the statement, "People who are trying to impress everyone with how much they know usually only impress themselves" It is a form of arrogance that places one above the other, at least in his own mind. This is not affective ministry. One forgets the purpose of ministry.

Again, let us learn from the example of Jesus, "... the Son of man did not come to be ministered unto, but to minister..." (St. Matthew 20:28). Although the gospel message in the same, the presentation is what makes the difference. The bible says, "...he that winneth souls is wise..." (Proverbs 11:30).

The failure of ministry takes place because the messenger may well be aware of what the message is, but does know to whom the message is being presented. Again, look at the ministry of Jesus. He knew the mind-set of the people and when He preached He used parables; simply stories that the common man understood.

The Apostle James states, "If a brother or sister be naked, and destitute of daily food, And one of you say unto them, 'Depart in peace, be ye warmed and filled'; notwithstanding ye give them not those things which are needful to the body; what doth it profit?" (James 2:15-16) You cannot effectively minister to a hungry man without feeding him first.

When ministering one must ask oneself the question; "Is what I am saying or the tactic I'm using relevant?" Of course the Gospel always is, but, "Am I presenting it in a way that the people can relate to? Do I present myself as a humble messenger to the people or as a condemner wrapped in self-righteousness?"

I worked for a Christian publishing company which published books and gospel tracts. Among the tracts was one called "Here's a Tip" designed for waitresses in restaurants. Instead of leaving money for the waitress Christians would leave this gospel tract to share the message of Christ. However, the company soon received a number of letters from waitresses and restaurant owners asking them to stop publishing these tracts because many people were leaving these instead of money, and because waitresses often relied upon tips to help their income, they felt that they were being cheated. This made the Christian appear to be cheap misers, hence, making the message ineffective.

THE CULTURE IN THE HOOD

Ministering within the Hood, or the community surrounded by drugs, violence, and gangs is not the same as ministering to the community with less violence. The way of "survival" is often the way of the "hood".

I recall seeing a documentary on TV a number of years ago on the subject of young gang members, some of them as young as 8 and 10 years old. Most of these had already dropped out of school, were being raised by a single parent; usually the mother, and had seen many of their peers die violently to gang warfare.

The saddest thing I remember was an interview with an 8 year old boy who said he did not expect to live to see adulthood and had seen a number of his young friends killed. While most young boys had ambitions of growing up and one day playing ball or becoming architect, or having a role model to pattern themselves after, their desire was to be part of a gang and carry a pistol.

The trophy of these youth was to have an expensive pair of gym shoes worn by a famous athlete, even though the shoes costs more than any of them had. Some were even willing to kill for the shoes and fight if anyone stepped on or scuffed them. Although many of these youth were in their early teens they had experienced enough of hard life to put them in a much higher age mentality. How do we minister to these young people?

How would Jesus minister to them? Let's go back to His time and see an example. There is a core in every person that, although they live in a different environment, they have basic emotions and needs. The core of man each is nurtured by his surroundings. Jesus' disciple, Peter was not in a gang of sorts, but he had a leadership personality as well as a temper. His upbringing and occupation as a fisherman brought out certain traits as well as passions. He seemed certain of himself and was not going to back down to any man. Peter would fight and although much is made of his denial of Jesus, it should be remembered that in the Garden of Gethsemane he did fight, cutting off a man's ear (St. John 18:10).

He would have fit in perfect in the hood, possibly even being a gang leader. He had the leadership quality. He had the temper and quite possibly would have been intolerant. He had the business sense to set up what drug dealers refer to as an "enterprise"

The first thing Jesus says to Peter is, "Follow me and I will make you a fisher of men" (St. Matthew 4:19) He relates to what Peter does for a living. He uses what Peter is familiar with to simplify his purpose. If Peter was a 21st century gang-leader in the hood He might have said, "Follow me and instead of destroying men I will show you how to build them"

When Jesus performs the miracle of the great catch of fish (St. Luke 5:1-10) Peter is not only astonished but convicted. He sees the light of Jesus and when comparing it to himself he feels unworthy to stand before the Lord. He confesses of being a sinner. "Depart from me; for I am a sinful man O Lord" (v.8) Jesus does not condemn him or reprimand him for his sinful lifestyle. But He gives him purpose; "… henceforth thou shalt catch men" (v.10)

When Jesus called Matthew (St. Matthew 9:9) he calls him from a job that was despised by the Jews. He was a tax collector for the oppressive Roman government and was considered a sell-out by the people. Most tax collectors were dishonest and Matthew hung out with dishonest friends. But he is so elated that Jesus called him until he made a supper for Jesus and invited all of his friends (St. Matthew 9:10-13). The whole gang was there, the house was filled with all of Matthew's friends, all of them known for their dishonest reputations and there sat Jesus in the middle of them. The religious leaders had a problem with it. They ask His disciples, "...Why eateth your master with publicans and sinners?"

The modern day comparison would have been equivalent to Jesus sitting and eating with gang members possibly even drug dealers. Not only did the religious leaders of that day have problem with it, some of the modern day ministers would have a problem with it. Yet the response form Jesus is still the same, "They that are whole need not a physician, but they that are sick" (v.12)

In every case Jesus never went among what many considered undesirables with a condemning message, but a message of hope and to show them that they were just as important to Him and any other person.

The same message should be ministered in the hood. Many of them have already been deemed worthless, by the media, the middle and upper class, and even some of the churches. Some that go in to minister do so in the same manner as the Missionaries that went to minister to Native Americans, with a sense of arrogance, feeling everything about them is hopeless, not understanding their culture and calling them stupid. Just like the Missionaries were non-affective among the Nes Perce, so it appears many are non-affective in the hood.

THE RELEVANCE OF THE GOSPEL

The Gospel has not nor will it ever change. It is the Word of God and He never changes. "For I am the LORD, I change not... (Malachi 3:6) The Word is true and the minister must be fully convinced of this and preach it with conviction.

In all of mankind's existence there has never been an atheistic culture (there have been atheistic governments. But even they could not suppress or stop the movement of the gospel throughout their nations) Religion is as old as time. But even religion alone cannot change the hearts of men. It is designed to change men from the outside and put it inside with rules, philosophies and teachings. The Word of God however, has always been relevant because it changes men from the inside out.

Jesus did not come to start another religion. If religion alone could have saved mankind it never would have been necessary for Jesus to come. It is flawed, has created wars, slavery, self-righteousness, made some feel better than others. The first murder committed (Cain killed his brother Abel) was over a difference of religious practice. It still has the same flaws today as wars are still fought, murders are still committed, rapes still occur, all in the name of religion.

Jesus asked his disciples, "Whom do men say that I am? (St. Matt.16:13). He did not ask this question because He was concerned with popular opinion or what people necessarily thought of Him, but the questions had a deeper purpose. He was about to reveal Himself to the world as to who he was and His purpose. The response was similar to what religions say about Jesus today; a prophet, one of the prophets of old, great teacher. If you asked the major religions today who Jesus was they'd all say similar things, prophet, messenger, teacher, a reincarnation of an older prophet.

"But whom say ye that I am?" is the question he posed to his disciples. The response of Peter was deeper than religion. It was greater than what religion could ever do. The response was a revelation inspired by God Himself.

"Thou art the Christ, the Son of the living God"

Every religion does not believe this or teach it. Even within Christianity there are certain organizations, denominations and cults that deny this. Jesus said, "Upon this rock I will build my Church..."

The "Rock" was not Peter, but the revelation that Peter received from God, "Jesus is the Christ" Although there are many that fall under the religious category of Christianity, not believing that Jesus is the Christ means that they are not a part of the Church. Many are religious, belong to an organization, even acknowledge Jesus one way or another but are not part of the Church.

Although the cultures are different, the message is the same. The Gospel is the Good News that Jesus Christ has redeemed mankind from his sin.

CHAPTER SEVEN

THE CHURCH OUTSIDE THE WALLS

Andrew J. Latchison

My religious "stand" was based primarily on the fact that my Mother said that God needed representatives, bold soldiers for the His kingdom. I was always to be a witness for the Lord; to live so God could use me anytime and anywhere. She reiterated every chance she got that Jesus said "If I was ashamed of Him, He would be ashamed to own me before His Father, in Heaven."

So, that's what I did. I took a stand; in my "hood," on the streets, and at my school. Oh, how I remember those ridiculous classroom parties for every holiday;

especially, Christmas, Valentine's Day, St. Patrick's Day, and many of my fellow classmate's birthday parties. There was always a party that I was excluded from. I would hear the Temptations singing, *My Girl* and *Psychedelic Shack*; the Jackson Five *I Want You Back*, and *ABC*, and, Sly and the Family Stone *Thank You for Letting Me Be Myself Again*! I could hear the rants and the raving, the infectious laughter through the door.

You see, my teacher (s) Ms. Bess, Ms. Moore, or Ms. Bush would graciously put my desk outside in the hallway and close the door. I insisted that it was "against my religion to dance." The teacher or some appointed classmate would open the door, oh, so slightly, and set a paper plate on the desk with a hot dog, ketchup and mustard, and corn curls or popcorn. After a short while, the door would open again and a cup of punch would seemingly be shoved out to me. It was done so swiftly, some of the punch would be spilled on the desk or onto the floor. It was like all of a sudden, someone would remember, "Andrew doesn't have a napkin."

That's the story of my life—not ever really "fitting in" but seeking attention any way I could. I found out over the years that there are scores of spiritual, religious aliens who are intentionally ignored and overlooked by "undercover agents" who inadvertently shut out the different, the dissident, and the derelict. Desks are pushed into the hallway of life; it's the sad, surreal scenario of the church and its relationship with the streets. The Church will not be taken seriously until it adopts an initiative that is passionate and persuasive.

The "urban initiative" must be contained, moreover, within the periphery of the predicament —the evasive, problematic procurement of the issues. In other words, do we know what the "real" problems are; or, do we assume to know by our visual assessments of what appears to be the challenges. In addition, are we equipped to present efficacious essentials for progress and advancements; or, are we causing a systemic embellishment to appease our guilt for the lack of causation.

Our Neanderthal approach is only secondary to our dysfunctional discourse of a deliberate disassociation and/or disconnection from the apparent. We know what the problem is. It is our animosity for who we claim to be the impetus of our evangelistic thrust. We have removed ourselves from the antipathy of the crimes, violence, and even the ignorance of the ghetto, the hood, the community. I have often heard it said that "those derelicts are losers. They don't want to do better; they just want a hand- out. They are satisfied with who they are and where they are. They do nothing but tear up, tear down, ruin whatever they are given."

There is an associative paradigm that totally negates the possibilities of the urban disenfranchised. The excuse for debate is "what are WE supposed to do if they don't want any help, if they don't want to be saved?" So, to qualify our attempt to assist, we initiate a forum of consortiums and conferences; we propose self-help programs. We establish clothes closets, food pantries, turkey times, summer retreats, and Christmas baskets as if to pacify our professed mission and evangelistic ministries.

Many external ministries are reluctant to become apparent or obvious in the 'hoods because of the subversive attitude of the traditional (local) churches. If there is a welcome, an "olive branch" extended by the church, it is to reassign the value of the "outside" ministry, to steal the Work, the "first responders" of the Work. The "we" or "us" embrace is devalued by the "I" or "my" local entitlement. You see, Faith-Based Initiative funding, grants, are the motivation of many pretentious, hypocritical personas that appear to do outreach. It is a facade that facilitates a forum.

If only there wasn't a polarization of those called to the highways and hedges, the 'HOOD!' Why would there even be a disconnection, a disparity between any religious entities, folk of the 'Household of Faith?' Shouldn't we want to seek to save souls for Christ, to build the Kingdom of God one soul at a time, together? What is the problem?

The song says, "How to reach the masses, men of every birth, for an answer Jesus gave the key; He said, if I, if I be lifted up from the Earth, I'll draw all men unto me." Regardless of the earthly source, isn't Jesus the author and the finisher of our faith? Isn't He the reason for all seasons? Let's let Him have it! He would never sit us outside in the hallway, away from the BIG PARTY, the celebration of life in Him!

Jesus said, "I came not into the world to condemn the world but that the world through me might be saved." Prejudice, bias, racism, ignorance, arrogance, indifference, and unforgiveness have created distance- the disenfranchisement. What happened to our knowledge of the love of Jesus? Everybody has a place of need, want, brokenness, a weakness in life. The Church must realize that every man would be changed, healed, and transformed, if and when WE do the Work, regardless of who gets the credit; to bring the lost to Christ. You see ministering to the "men of every birth" is not about better and bigger programs (ministries); it is about better and stronger relationships.

This present mind-set may require a paradigm shift in how we, our churches, and ministries reach the community. Much of what we have done is sit the desk outside the room, and shove a little food, a little refreshment (relief) out and around. Our extensions have been based on events, activities, and programs. If we are going to have an effective approach, it starts with feeling pressure, compassion in our soul for the deliverance of souls.

Again, Jesus said he came to preach Good News to the poor, to proclaim liberty to them that are bound, recovery of sight to the blind, and release to the oppressed. Jesus' intent is to transform us from what we are to what we will become. God wants workers who will lose themselves and their ambitions and will go to any measure, by any means necessary to bring others to Christ. There is power in our working together to reach men and to bring them to safety, to love, to the Lord. There is power in sharing the load, shouldering the weight.

God's work is to be done in the "hall." Yes, it is done in the hallway of mankind, in the community. Yes, I want to change my philosophical stance. The placement in the hallway is a transfer of appeal, the transition, a shift in outreach. Take the PARTY, the CELEBRATION into the hallway!

In my study, I have learned that the average non-churched person seeks to know a number of Christians and hear the Gospel preached a number of times before they will believe the message. This means it entails cooperation; a collaboration, a conglomerate of Christians reaching "out", together. We are in a challenge much larger than ourselves, the church where truly; "everybody is somebody and Christ is all." Our place is not the only locale of the Lord where we are invited to "come over here where the table is spread and the feast of the Lord is going on." For some, it's their "Holy Ghost headquarters." No, we must eventually; no, now realize that the battle will only be won when WE work, together- suburban and urban, not in isolation.

Yes, attention needs to be directed to the hallway. Things are actively going strong in the "classroom" but much of the energy must be redirected to the displaced and, again, the disenfranchised. The focus of evangelism suffers from an amnestic condition. Hundreds of thousands of the non-churched are former patrons. For whatever reason, these are they who have walked away disappointed, dismayed, disillusioned, discouraged—"dissed" and hurt, wounded many times by "friendly fire." Spiritual operatives have socially ignored them simply because they assume eventually they'll be back.

Noise in the hallway—peril, trouble, trials, lack, grief, generally moves the "desk" back into the classroom. With the pressures we all face, those who have left us could eventually be the catalyst, the cure, and the help for all of us.

Whether we are the minister or the one who needs ministering (to), we have to be cognizant of that very appeal- ministry. The Scriptures declare, "The harvest is ripe (ready) but the laborers are few." Why then, is there this shortage of workers? I dare say, we are getting the illustration but we are missing the point! The need is at the point of origin. It's always been, and always has been the delusion of the Church.

We're so busy focusing on the credibility of evangelism or the cry to legitimize the need for urban evangelism that we miss it! The cry is from within. The travail, the origin of the ill is internal; and, therein is the process, the development of true outreach. "For the time has come that judgment must begin at the House of God," (1Peter 4:17). How could we have missed it? Why do we consistently point the finger, pass the buck, and shift the blame? "Who's going to take the blame? Who will bear the shame?" Well, all of us should!

I say, "If walls could talk and if shoes could tell where some of our feet have been, there are a lot of folks wouldn't be as holy as they look." We, yes, WE are many times the perpetrators of the fraud. We fall prey to the devil's ploy, schemes, devices, distractions, delusions, and diversions.

We push people out by principle and pull others in by pretense. We only need them as a number for our quota, to show our level of growth while not even putting a dent in the status of the Lost. We fail to realize, WE are the "hood;" it is US who need the ministry—the ministers who need ministering. The "Reach" is not beyond US. It is indelibly, obviously US! We think that we're doing God a favor by reaching the lost but in most cases, we are the culprits. Those who are in the "hallway" belong in the Big Picture, the scheme of things, if you will. Through no fault of their own, many have been exiled, excommunicated, placed in the "X" files, when they are the ones who offer the solution to our ills, our deception. We are the sinners who have been saved by Grace through Faith, and, "that not of ourselves…"

When we eliminate the division and the disparity in the distance placed between us, we can affect

Evangelism. Through the eyes of Christ, we evoke the love, the compassion, the passion for souls; we see the ills. Jesus tells us to "Go wash in the pool of Siloam...," for it is then that we see our reflection, the image of another who needs deliverance, healing.

Yes, the Lord wants us to GO, then, wash with familiarity, a reality of purpose. You see, it is then, and then only that we realize the similitude. The "hungry" don't want the hot dogs and punch; they want the distance between US dissipated. They want a real understanding of their undeserved dilemma. Therein is our mantra, "Understanding is a wellspring of LIFE, to him that has it," (Proverbs 16:22).

The Apostle Peter said in Acts 2:38, "Repent and be baptized every one of you in the Name of Jesus Christ for the forgiveness of your sins, and you will receive the gift of the Holy Spirit." This same Apostle in the next chapter, Acts 3, traversed with John to the temple to pray when he was confronted with the "beggar challenge." Here was another one "kicked to the curb", kept out through no fault of his own. The beggar lay by the Gate called Beautiful asking alms of those who congregated for "praise and worship." Yes, the indictment was the same as it is today—the pews are full but the people are empty. You see, the congregants passed by the "church" on their way into the temple. The ministry, the desperate soul lay at the Gate, so close but yet so far away! "Give him a coin and then close the door," they said.

Peter looked at that man who was lame, impotent in his feet and declared in Acts 3:6, "Silver and gold have I none; but such as I have give I thee, in the Name of Jesus rise up and walk." You see, "Bubba", at the Gate is not concerned with our titles. He's addressed the other Bishops, Apostles, Prophets, Prophetesses, Pastors, Elders, Ministers, Evangelists, Missionaries, Worship Leaders, Praise Dancers, Sunday School teachers, Church Administrators, Deacons, Trustees, Stewards, and Stewardesses, and the First and Elect Ladies who have consistently passed him with the "Help," the cure for his ill.

He now gives attention to this man who stops, who regards Him! Peter offers him an alternative for his dilemma. What he really says is, "What you're looking for, you're looking at!" I offer you Jesus, your Savior and Healer if you'll accept Him. In the Name of JESUS, rise up and walk! The Bible said that the lame took Peter's hand, looked up, leaped up, stood up, and walked. He started shouting and praising God! Once healed, he went with them into the temple. They (the disenfranchised) don't care about WHO we are. They've met, encountered US all. They know US, about US; they are US! We need to extend a "such as we have," by any means necessary. There is a state of emergency!

It's all about the Love of Jesus! So, we need to "be" about it! Our Call is the cause of Christ. "For the World is hungry for the Living Bread; lift the Savior up for men to see. He said, if I, if I be lifted up from the Earth, I'll draw all men unto Me!" Yes, the Call for the evangel is the Commission of the Christ.

"Softly, and tenderly, Jesus is calling; calling for you and for me. Safe on the portals, He's waiting and watching: calling all sinners come Home". George Beverly Shea sang this invitation at the Billy Graham Crusade thousands of times. (Speaking of Billy Graham, he is the world's greatest Evangelist of our time, having led millions of souls to Christ). His consistent appeal was to offer Christ and his Good News, the Gospel. When Rev. Graham extended the Invitation to Discipleship, hundreds would move toward the altar for prayer.

"Jesus, I am a sinner. I confess my sin and ask you for forgiveness. Jesus, come into my heart and save me. I believe that you died, was resurrected, and you're coming back again for me. Thank you, Lord, for accepting me as your Own. Thank you, Lord, Amen."

Now, truly, wherever we are and whoever we are, that's all that really matters. That's all that we should remember! That should be our focus—JESUS, the author and the finisher of our Faith. He is ALL we need to offer. HE is ALL we have to give, regardless!

He says, "Come unto me all ye that labor and are heavy laden and I will give you rest. Whoever comes to me, I will in no wise cast out. I came not into the world to condemn the world, but that the world through ME might be saved!"

Yes, Bubba lies at the Gate, so close but yet, so far away. Andrew and Andria are stuck in the hallway through no fault of their own. And, Godfrey and Gladys are wandering aimlessly on the highways and in the hedges and must be compelled to come in.

Paul said in 1Cor.6:11, "And such were some of you: but you are washed, but you are sanctified, but you are justified in the name of the Lord Jesus, and by the Spirit of our God." Let's put aside our petty differences and lame excuses. WE must go out to escort "them" IN, giving US the glorious opportunity to come IN, also.

Now, the doors of the Church are open.

ALL are welcome!

CHAPTER EIGHT

SOULS IN PRISON

Richard R. Blake

MICHAEL'S STORY

I never want to go back; Michael declared. Never. The sign over the door reads Family Book Center. The symbol of the fish with Greek letters in the center implies and proclaims that this is a Christian bookstore. The store is situated on the border of urban Oakland, California and San Leandro a suburb and ministers to a cross section of urban and suburban cultures. However, the primary mission of the store is to provide books, Bibles, and educational curriculum supplies to the ethnic churches and their constituents throughout the urban community.

Michael came into the store asking for help. He had slept the night before outside at a nearby park. The cold wind and damp rain had chilled him to the bone. Two words, no three, were apparent from Michael's troubled eyes and trembling lips: "tired, cold, and lonely."

The concern for the homeless became more than an academic exercise; providing shelter for the homeless loomed before me as a practical life concern. It was an issue I needed to face in light of my personal values. My perception of "homelessness" took on a new meaning through an individual named Michael.

My decision to help Michael may never impact legislation, sway social reform, eliminate racism, eradicate poverty, or abolish the political corruption rampant in many urban communities, but it suddenly became crucial for me to find an answer to Michael's dilemma. I wanted to help him in some meaningful way. I wanted to demonstrate Christian concern, to make my actions consistent with my profession of faith. I wanted to be more intellectually honest and more practically credible. I determined to challenge the sophisticated, ethical, pharisaical, religious attitudes prevalent in society today.

As I begin to examine my own personal commitment and motivation in light of the Christian principles I championed, I begin to relate the moral responsibility of society to the small acts of kindness we exercise individually. I was awakened to a need for being spiritually relevant while being socially realistic. I immediately put action into my decision and picked up the phone. I knew of an agency that ministers to the physical and spiritual needs of the people like Michael. I contacted the organization and provided Michael with detailed information and the address of the center.

Two weeks later Michael returned. Again, he was seeking help. He told me of the drug and alcohol free policy at the center and the need to conform to the "house rules." Michael was not ready to accept the warmth and comfort offered by the community; he chose to live a life of non-conformity and returned to the streets.

Because of an environment of crime, poverty, family abandonment and a dysfunctional childhood, Michael felt overwhelmed, overstretched, and unable to take control of his life. At the age of twelve Michael was verbally abused and physically beaten. He was abandoned by his parents, his schooling was interrupted, and he became severely handicapped academically.

Michael told me of his dependence on alcohol. Today it was obvious that he had been drinking. He had reached a point of desperation accompanied by a spirit of penitence and a determination to clean up his life.

A month or more passed before I saw Michael again. He had been picked up, by the police, drunk and was charged with disorderly conduct while aimlessly wandering the streets. Michael had just been released from 30 days in the county jail. Now he was outside, free again and determined not to go back.

Alcohol-free, Michael stood taller, his eyes brighter, his smile broader. Filled with hope, Michael had reached another milestone as he resolved to take charge, to begin a new life. However, Michael was again, homeless.

Michael's experience is a familiar story to those growing up in the inner-city. Alcoholic parents and an abusive childhood increase the propensity toward addictions and lead to a repeated cycle of alcohol, and abuse. Our inter-cities are in crisis. Michael's story is repeated over and over again in urban areas across America, already plagued with violence, felonies, drug arrests, poverty, and racial disparity.

Richard R. Blake

MINISTRY TO THE INCARCERATED

Nearly 50 percent of all crimes are committed by people on parole or probation. Public agencies, parole experts, police department officials, and concerned volunteers have developed programs to teach parolees about life outside the prison walls. These programs aim to cut recidivism.

Local, state, and federal government administrators are working with researchers and study groups in an attempt to find solutions to this ongoing, out of control problem. Community service organizations are proactive in providing skills training, self-worth affirmation, and other activities for high-risk youth in our cities in hopes of preventing crime.

There are approximately one and one-half million men and women incarcerated in this country. The emphasis of the American prison system has vacillated between punishment for crime and rehabilitation of the individual offender. The staggering rate of recidivism and the number of repeat offenders indicate that prisoners are not being reformed. A crowded prison population, escalating prison maintenance costs, and state budget cuts have led to early release of prisoners, increasing the numbers of men and women on probation and parole, creating additional grounds for concern.

Studies show that a program cannot be assured of success in rehabilitating an inmate until there has been an inner change that produces a positive resolve, reconciliation, and regeneration. The apostle Paul put it this way: "Therefore if any man be in Christ, he is a new creature: old things are passed away; behold all things are become new." (2 Corinthians 5:17)

Regeneration must accompany rehabilitation. It is the challenge and calling of the chaplain and the Christian volunteer to bring the redemptive message of the cross of Christ, new life, and hope to those behind prison walls.

My friend Glenn Morrison, president of Follow Up Ministries, International, a ministry to men and women behind bars shares this story.

> One Sunday afternoon, as we drove away from San Quentin prison in the San Francisco Bay area, a business man accompanying me posed this question. "Do you ever get discouraged? You had 35 men in your seminar session today out of a prison population of over 3,000." [I] responded, No, our job is to work with the Christian inmates, training them to go back into their cellblocks as ambassadors of Jesus Christ. It is their responsibility to evangelize San Quentin. Our Seminars in Christian Discipleship are designed to train those behind prison walls to become disciple makers as they follow the principles modeled by the Apostle Paul during his prison experience.

Jesus commissioned his disciples to go and to make disciples. In ministering to inmates we must go with the idea of equipping them to become disciples of Jesus, showing them how to follow Christ, sending them back into their living units to represent Him to their peers.

The Christian prisoner has the opportunity to be "a light in a dark place." By comparing the ministry and the position of the believer in your church with the believer in prison you will realize that the role in ministry is identical. This life change and spiritual equipping also readies the inmate to return to family life and as a productive member of the community.

Churches today have the opportunity to establish ministry teams and partnerships with jail and prison chaplains to bring the message of light and life in Jesus Christ to these prisoners still living in spiritual darkness.

As you contemplate teaming with your church, local prison chaplains or a faith based prison ministry it is important that you envision what you want to accomplish in your personal outreach ministry to the: incarcerated, parolee , or individuals on probation.

In addition to visiting the prison and teaming with the chaplain in Bible studies, chapel services, evangelism, and discipleship ministry, there are other opportunities for service. Providing literature, devotionals, writing letters of encouragement, prayer, phone calls, and inmate visitation are important additional open doors of service.

Most churches and their members have had little contact with the incarcerated men and women who populate our prisons and jails and are unenlightened about life behind bars. It is important that for ministry to be effective we understand the debilitation and brokenness experienced by those caught up in the cycle of discouragement, debasement and defeat.

Only as we identify with their emotions, circumstances, and environment can we establish a realistic opportunity for "responsive evangelism." We must demonstrate sincerity and genuine concern to move beyond conversion to develop maturity and meet the spiritual needs of the inmate, including: counseling and encouragement in areas of spiritual, mental, and emotional stability.

You may be apprehensive about getting involved in prison ministry because of a fear of the unknown as a result of Hollywood movies, perceived stereotypes, media reports, a lack of understanding, or fear of personal safety. While these are legitimate concerns, it is important to recognize that this is significant work and can be done effectively by participating with others in ministry teams.

PARENTS IN PAIN

It is estimated that there may be as many as 800,000 children in the United States who have a parent in prison. The influence and effect of incarceration of parents on their children cannot be minimized. The trauma of separation, the stigma of shame, and the economic implications on the remaining family members can be confusing and devastating to the child.

As the church and as individual Christians we must respond to the need and become more focused on ensuring that these children have a safe, permanent home, one that maintains and promotes their well-being. Churches and prison ministry organizations are targeting families of inmates and ex-inmates with programs to offset the immediate and long-term effect of incarceration on family members.

The Family is an institution designed by God. Today our family structure is being weakened by immorality, divorce, violence, and materialism. We live in troubled times. Influential liberal leaders and media moguls are mocking God and traditional family values. God is in the family repair business. He wants to strengthen family ties and bind families together.

There are practical steps we can take to bridge the gap between the inmate and their families. We can visit inmates in prison as they experience loneliness, guilt, and the hopelessness of their situation. We can respond to the needs of the offender or family by providing aid in particular matters and individual concerns.

The Illinois Department of Corrections sponsors a "Mom and Me Camp." This is a program that gives children a chance to bond with their incarcerated mother. Children ages, seven through twelve, participate in the three days of planned activities, at the correctional facility. Opportunities are planned for playing games, crafts, and quiet times together. These activities are designed to encourage communication and bonding not possible in the usual short visits. The children spend the evening with volunteers in traditional summer camp activities. This is only one example of creative ministries to provide a Christian presence in a critical area of need.

We can provide resources and information to these families as well as establishing and maintaining relationships with the parents and their children. It is critical to establish and communicate an environment of trust in these relationships as well as to break the cycle of crime by changing the hearts and minds of the incarcerated and the family members, including the children. The message of Christ is more than another community program.

Even hardened criminals can be touched and changed by the power of the gospel. Returning the ex-offender to the home instead of prison is of extreme importance for these young people. Recidivism studies reveal that on-going participation in faith based community programs is an important element in reducing "re-offense." Discipleship training implemented by mentors is an effective means of restoring inmates into productive and responsible parental roles.

Scripture exhorts us to visit those in prison. The writer of the book of Hebrews encourages the reader to: "Remember those who are in prison, as though you were in prison with them." (Hebrews 13:3)

Chaplains and religious volunteers encounter situations which uncover dormant beliefs, deeply rooted feelings and emotions that lie suppressed just below the surface. It is important for the volunteer to be sensitive to the emotional roller coaster experienced by the newly incarcerated.

Stresses and tensions need to be dealt with. Personal guilt, anger, self-contempt, depression, and family situations take on a new dimension for the prisoner. Negative attitudes, hopelessness, and despair face the incarcerated on a daily basis. The basic human needs of an inmate within the prison environment must be understood if we are to minister to these complex social and personal issues.

Researchers have often ignored religion in their studies of the social sciences. Considering the scope of prison ministry it is ironic that religious factors have been overlooked as significant deterrents to inmate unrest, uncontrolled discipline and recidivism.

Religious instruction is one of several rehabilitate disciplines. It is the only approach that addresses the root problem, a moral or sin crisis inside the prisoner. Studies now show that inmates often seek God to help deal with prison life.

An insight into the unique challenges of the prison community is imperative for effective service and ministry. We must expand our perception of the correctional process if we are to be effective in ministry to the inmate. If we are to minister to the prison community it is important that we observe prison life through the eyes of those who live there.

CHAPLAINS ENLIST CHURCH PRISON MINISTRY TEAMS

Churches today have the opportunity to establish ministry teams and partnerships with jail and prison chaplains to bring the message of light and life in Jesus Christ to those still living in spiritual darkness behind prison walls. Most churches and their members have had little contact with people in prisons and remain unenlightened about them.

As you contemplate teaming with local prison chaplains it is important that you envision what you want to accomplish in your church outreach or personal team efforts. You can begin by comparing the ministry and the position of the believer in your church with the believer in prison to realize the role in ministry is identical.

Jesus challenged, or commanded us to go and to make disciples. In ministering to inmates we must go with the idea of equipping them to become disciples of Jesus, showing them how to follow Christ, sending them back into their living units to represent Him to their peers. Each Christian prisoner has the opportunity to be "a light in a dark place."

In addition to visiting the prison and teaming with the chaplain in Bible studies, chapel services, evangelism, and discipleship ministry, there are other opportunities for service. Providing literature, devotionals, writing letters of encouragement, and prayer, phone calls, and inmate visitation are important additional open doors of service. These suggestions provide for a relationship to develop, and to access the sincerity, maturity and spiritual need of the inmate. You are then ready to offer advice and encouragement.

You may be apprehensive about getting involved in prison ministry because of a fear of the unknown as a result of Hollywood movies you have seen, perceived stereotypes, media reports, a lack of understanding, or fear of personal safety. While these are legitimate concerns it is important to recognize this is very significant work and can be done effectively by participating with others in ministry teams. Contact your local chaplain to explore opportunities available locally.

Studies show that a program cannot be assured of success in rehabilitating an inmate until there has been an inner change that produces a positive permanent and personal renewal. Old outlooks and attitudes disappear. We experience a conversion. Once we realize the new relationship we have in Christ our practices will begin to correspond to our position. God is looking for our unconditional surrender.

ALTERNATIVES TO INCARCERATION – RESTORATIVE JUSTICE

FIFTY DOLLAR REPAIR VERSUS A LIFE OF CRIME

He vaulted himself to the top of the six-foot fence. Like a high wire performer, he balanced himself. A tall tree at the end of the property line gave promise of access to the roofs of the row of business buildings facing Mac Arthur Boulevard.

The strong branches reached across the small gap between the fence and the building. He moved lithely along the rooftop staying in the shadows. Adrenaline kicked in. He crept forward. His goal was the skylight on the next to the last store building on the street.

He stealthily moved toward his goal. He was there now. A dog barked. He froze; waited, and then he crept toward the skylight. Crouching he looked down. He smashed the window. Glass shattered. The dog barked again.

Neighbors had just turned off the TV; each evening they watched the 10 o'clock news on channel two. The dog barked. He sounded agitated. Curious, they looked out the window. In the moonlight, silhouetted on the roof of the Christian bookstore, they saw the young man. They dialed 911.

Red and blue lights flashed. He lay flat, afraid to breathe. Within minutes the teenager was secure in the custody of San Leandro police officers. I had become the victim of a crime.

Restorative Justice provides an alternative to incarceration: a focus is put on the harms of the wrongdoing, rather than on the rules or laws broken. It is the vision of Restorative Justice to encourage collaboration and reintegration rather than coercion and isolation. This philosophy maintains that restoring injuries is the first of three basic premises on which a criminal justice system should be based. This involves the victim, the community, and he offender. Full involvement of all three is important for the success of the process.

The government is accountable for safeguarding law and order. The community is responsible to create and preserve right relationships, reconciliation, and reintegration. Sentencing low-risk inmates to community service and work programs allows them to maintain a productive vocation to support their families, and pay restitution to their victims.

In retrospect it is interesting to note, the attempted break in of my bookstore was my introduction to Restorative Justice. I did not know the term nor expect to experience the benefits.

I later learned that the juvenile authorities had worked with my landlord, the insurance company, and the offender. The young man made restitution by paying the expense of the window replacement. This was his first offense. Supervision and probation arrangements within the county of Alameda kept this young offender from detention at the California Youth Authority, perhaps saving him from becoming another statistic in the cycle of crime, prison, release, a repeated offence and the beginning of another cycle of recidivism.

PROACTIVE PROGRAMS FOR REACHING AT RISK YOUTH

CRIME PREVENTION AND REDUCING RECIDIVISM

Concerned individuals, public agencies, and faith based ministries are formulating and implementing proactive programs involving community wide efforts in reaching at risk youth.

Michigan's Van Buren County Sheriff recently coached a high school varsity baseball team. By teaching good citizenship and providing this example of leadership Sheriff Gribler established a unilateral bridge to forming a better working environment between the community and the laws enforcement officers serving them. Other communities nationwide are establishing similar volunteer programs and activities for reaching troubled youth.

Rehabilitation programs within the correctional facilities are aimed at job training and self-management skills. These efforts also assist former prisoners find organizations that can help them transition back into society. An information sharing exchange, also provides parolees and those on probation with data on training programs, available housing and employment opportunities. Recruiting active participation from local business and industry leaders is another important step in the re-entry process. The correctional facilities in your county may provide volunteers opportunities to serve in this process.

PRISON MINISTRY - STEPS FOR INVOLVEMENT

Christian volunteers visiting in the prison and in homes bring a message of hope to the inmates and their families. We have the opportunity of evangelism and discipleship. We must not be distracted from ministering the good news of healing to the broken hearted, deliverance to those in bondage, release to the oppressed and light to the blind.

The first step to take is a prayerful examination of your motives. God wants a wholehearted dedication and a singleness of purpose from His followers. The volunteer minister to prison inmates is entering into an arena of spiritual battle. It is important to count the cost. Examine this in light of the impact on your family and friends. Recognize that the commitment in time alone will involve sacrifice. Be sure your family is behind you in your decision. You must be motivated by a love for hurting, misunderstood, often dysfunctional, and rebellious individuals.

Each of you is reading this book for a different reason. Some of you may have loved ones who are or have been incarcerated. God may have put a burden on your heart to help others who are going through these experiences, or you may want to reach out to other inmates to repay what someone did for your loved one.

Others of you may have been introduced to prison ministry through the visiting room of a prison or jail. Maybe you were incarcerated yourself and now have a call to reach out to the hurting men and women behind the walls. You may have the gift of evangelism and feel called to use this gift to reach prisoners with the gospel message. Whatever your motive, it is important to recognize the cost in time commitment.

It is important for you to understand your strengths, gifts, skills, interests and desires to decide which volunteer ministry you are best suited for. This will help you best use your talents, time, and energy as you assume responsibilities that will be a blessing to others and bring a sense of reward and satisfaction to you personally.

Next you will want to identify the correctional facilities in your area. For example, in Alameda County, in California, we have Santa Rita County Jail, Juvenile Hall, Duel Vocational Institute, and city jails in each of the major cities in the county.

In large population areas you may find several classifications. There may be city jails, county jails, juvenile facilities, state and federal prisons. Each of these facilities serves a different and unique roll in the field of corrections. Opportunities for ministry will vary in line with the needs and offerings of the Office of Volunteer Services or the Chaplains in charge.

In larger institutions it will be necessary to contact the Director of Volunteer Services to find out what opportunities are available. You may in turn be referred to the Chaplain's office for service in Christian ministry. You will then be provided with the necessary application forms and told of any additional requirements for volunteering. In most cases it will be necessary to attend some prerequisite orientation training.

The next step is to align yourself with an organization that will provide you with an open door of service. There are many national and local organizations using volunteers in the work of prison ministry. Visit the inter-net for a listing. Prison Fellowship, Match II, and Friends Further Out are just a few of the ministries you will find. Your church may have its own jail and prison ministry.

I have personally been involved with Follow Up Ministries, Inc. of Castro Valley, California. This group was founded by Glenn L. Morrison in 1956 and has branches in several cities throughout the United States. FUMI provides regular opportunities for training and orientation in working with the inmates in correctional facilities. After the initial orientation, a plan of mentoring takes the volunteer a step further. Opportunity is given to work alongside a trained volunteer in reaching those behind the prison walls.

While rehabilitation and religion play an important role in the life of many prisoners, there is no substitute for God's work of regeneration. It is the challenge and calling of the chaplain and the Christian volunteer to bring the redemptive message of the cross of Christ, new life, and hope to those behind the prison's walls. We are called to introduce the inmate to the claims of the Gospel and to Jesus Christ personally.

Prison ministry is unique. It is a ministry of careful listening and compassionate healing. We must be careful to withhold judgment. By ministering to the incarcerated we can help individuals discover forgiveness and reconciliation through God's love. The church can provide channels of communication within both the local and the prison communities.

The testimonies of those who visit the incarcerated are consistently warm reports of inmates eager to have contact with the world beyond the walls and eager to learn principles that will help them take a stronger stand in their walk with the Lord. As you minister to an inmate you multiply your ministry as he/she returns to the cellblock to evangelize and disciple others.

WHERE DO WE GO FROM HERE?

Inner city churches plagued with the plight of the poor, struggling with hunger, deprivation, human inequality, increased crime on neighboring streets, rampant drug trafficking, and drive by shootings have been compelled to discontinue most of their evening programs, and install locked security gates on fenced in parking lots.

The church is "No longer the light of the world." (Matthew 5:14 KJV) The church has lost its influence on the city, and is but a darkened shadow of its past impact on issues of social injustice, racial disparity, and political corruption.

It is time that we move from the sanctuary to the street, trading our traditional theology for the life giving powerful message of the Gospel of Christ to impact urban America by our living example.

We need to translate the principle truth of our faith into spiritual applications through implementing the Christ-centered paradigm of the Urban Apologetic. Only as we leave the safe haven of our chapels, sanctuaries, and store front churches can we expect to become an accepted influence in the community, turning a cycle of rebellion, disrespect, and mockery to a cycle of revival, regeneration and reverence toward God.

Chapter Nine

We All Need

Joyce A. Graham

When I reflect on my own personal experience, during my early years, in the organized church, the lyrics of a song come to mind. The song is simply entitled, "We All Need" by Bryan Duncan. Following are some key verses (paraphrased) that have impacted me:

> I was raised with the lessons and the victory speech, As I fought for standards that I could not reach, And I'd hold my tongue, though the pain was great, And I covered my tears as we'd celebrate, While a private war raged with the fear and the doubt, Then I tried to run faster to find a way out I was convinced that if I stumbled they'd just cast me aside, Mock at my weakness and shatter my pride. 'Cause I've watched as they stoned the

more hesitant soul. But we all must remember, It's still
God's grace we all need...*

The lyrics of that song describe what many new
converts who come "off the streets" have experienced
within the four walls of the physical church during the
era in which I first became a Christian. We claimed
that we were victorious, even when we were not. We
were held to man-made standards that the person who
created the standards could not reach themselves. We
were convinced that if we were experiencing adversity
in our lives; perhaps it was because we were not doing
enough, that somehow it was our fault. So we would
try harder; run faster. If we would just pray more;
if we would just fast longer or more often, then "this
would not have happened to us."

Then we were encouraged to confess our faults and
shortcomings, only to become the subject of messages
from the pulpit and held up as examples for the "don't
let this happen to you" scenarios. And though we
were hurting, we were fearful that any display of
emotions, other than positive, superficial ones, would
be dissected and ultimately labeled as defeat. So we
learned to wear a facade as we joined the millions of
silent sufferers in the house of God.

In April, 1973, on Easter Sunday Morning, I gave my
life to the Lord. Looking back, I had no idea that when

I got up that morning, anything out of the ordinary would occur.

In fact, the only reason that I was going to church was because my sister had invited me and it was Easter. If you know anything at all about the African-American community and culture, you know that there are two days that you attend church—whether you are a Christian or not. That is on Easter and on Mother's Day. Not attending church on those two days is considered extremely irreverent and sacrilegious.

So, after a Saturday night of drinking and clubbing, I finally made it home sometime before dawn. I slept for a few hours, and then got up Sunday morning to get myself and my nine month old baby ready for church. My other little girl, who was two years old, was at her grandma's. As I waited for my sister to pick us up, I began to dread the whole ordeal. I was not particularly anxious or excited about church. I just wanted to get it over with and get on with my life.

At the conclusion of the service, the preacher made an appeal or altar call. He went on and on, and the longer he made the appeal, the more firmly I sat in my seat. With my baby in my arms and sitting there rather defiantly, I refused to budge an inch. I began to feel very agitated and extremely uncomfortable. Finally, he stopped and I breathed a heavy sigh of relief. Suddenly, I looked out of the corner of my eye and saw my sister. She had gotten up from where she had been sitting and was coming toward me with her hands extended. When she reached me, she took the baby from my arms. I felt myself rising from my seat, and then moving my legs until I was all the way in the front of the church. I invited the Lord into my life and received the gift of salvation that very day.

I felt the love of the saints immediately. However, something was missing; I could not put my finger on it nor could I articulate it back then. But now I know what it was; it was a lack of acceptance. After all, here was this skinny little black girl from the projects. I had just left the club the night before and I reeked of cigarettes and liquor. I was unchurched. I did not have the right clothes and came in wearing a micro-mini skirt. I had a huge Afro, bracelets going up and down my arms, and I had on earring hoops the size of saucers. But most of all I had just come off the streets and I had issues that could not be resolved with the right hand of fellowship.

In the midst of church folk who were second and third generation Christians and who had been in the church all their lives, there I was. I was only nineteen years old, with two little kids to support, and newly separated from my husband. My girls and I lived in the back room of my mom's house. I had not graduated high school and was on welfare. We lived in the red light district of St. Louis where prostitutes paraded up and down our street daily. I was not the typical church girl and I did not fit in. So when issues related to my old life began to surface, the church folk simply did not know how to respond.

My husband and I had been separated for several months. Initially, my estranged husband feigned interest and support of my new way of life. But after only a few months, he tried to persuade and influence me to defect from the faith. When I would not resort to my old way of living, he was no longer supportive of my transition and did everything he could think of to derail me. My resolve to remain steadfast in my commitment to God only made him angry.

One day he became engaged in a heated argument with an elderly relative. I quietly intervened in defense of the relative and suggested that he be more respectful. His wrath was immediately redirected toward me, and he struck me in the face, resulting in a serious black eye.

I was devastated and confused, because I was under the impression that since I had given my life to the Lord, I was immune to such abusive treatment. I consoled myself with the fact that I would soon be in the presence of the saints, which I so desperately needed during this time. However, when my Pastor and my relatives found out that I had a black eye, I was instructed to stay home and not be seen in public because of all of the negative connotations associated with a black eye.

Hurt and even more conflicted, I stayed away. One day, when I could no longer bear being away from the house of God, I got dressed, donned a pair of dark shades, and left for church. My presence at church was received with mixed reviews, but I did not care. I was able to endure the whispers and stares and receive the spiritual healing that I had not been able to obtain while at home in isolation.

In retrospect, I understand that the church was trying to protect me from embarrassment, but I suspect that it was they who were uncomfortable in the presence of someone who had (visibly) been a victim of domestic violence simply because they were not equipped to respond to domestic issues of that magnitude. They had only standard answers for victims of domestic violence or relational discord: They instructed wives to remain in abusive domestic environments in order to "keep the family together," they encouraged spouses to remain in marriages while their partner was blatantly engaged in adulterous, extramarital affairs, they instructed newly converted couples who had been living in "common law" to go home, pack, and separate sometimes totally uprooting or abandoning young, innocent children who were products of that relationship.

Let me hasten to add that I do not believe that the church should encourage, endorse, or condone sin. However, situations like the above example do not have a blanket, generic solution. Each situation is unique, and has to be addressed on a case by case basis.

For example, there was a couple who were living together without the benefit of ceremony. The Lord beautifully saved the young man. He went home and told his partner that he was saved, that he still loved her, but that there had to be an adjustment in the living arrangements. They both decided that they would remain in the same home, but maintain separate sleeping quarters. Although the arrangement was challenging and not at all ideal, they were able to successfully navigate through this difficult terrain. She eventually accepted Christ into her life, they were married, and seventeen years later, are still together and both are currently high ranking officials in the church.

I am aware that the example I cited above contains a lot of gray areas, and the solution may not have been ideal. But even in cases where scripture is crystal clear regarding an issue, religious leaders tend to err on the side of personal interpretation. Divorce and remarriage in the instance of fornication was granted by Jesus in St. Matthew 19:1-10. In cases such as that, where reconciliation is not possible, the innocent party has the right to obtain a divorce on the grounds of fornication and remarry.

My first husband and I never reconciled and finally divorced after I endured years of his numerous extramarital affairs and physical and emotional abuse. The Lord blessed me to meet and fall in love with a wonderful man. After we became engaged, my fiancé and I went to our Pastor who gave us his blessings. However, he alluded to the fact that because this would be my second marriage, he could not perform the ceremony. Furthermore, he stated that he could not allow the ceremony to take place in the church.

My fiancé and I were terribly disappointed, and made arrangements to be married at my sister's house. We sent an invitation to our pastor and his wife, but neither he nor his wife attended the ceremony. Although our pastor would not endorse our marriage, it was God ordained and we will soon be celebrating thirty-two wonderful years together.

After the Lord so beautifully saved me and turned my life around, I began to share my testimony with others. Particularly, how the Lord delivered me from several life threatening vices, such as smoking, drinking, drug experimentation, etc. Our church was invited to minister at a local prison. I was so excited and volunteered to share my testimony with the prisoners. When we arrived at the prison, my Pastor's wife discovered that I was to share my testimony. She pulled me aside and whispered something to the effect that I should "censor" my testimony. To this day, I am not sure of what her concerns were or what she thought I was going to share. I suspect that she did not want me to share certain aspects of my life before coming to the Lord. I was so hurt, that I very respectfully withdrew my request to give my testimony.

Instead, they allowed another young lady to sing a solo. I felt so frustrated that the prisoners did not have the opportunity to hear my testimony. I still feel to this very day that they would have benefitted and probably could have related to my testimony of being delivered from some of the vices that many of them perhaps struggled with and very possibly had contributed to their being incarcerated in the first place.

Please don't misunderstand me. I am not harboring resentment nor am I bitter regarding my negative encounters in the church. This is not a matter of the actions or inaction of the church or of the church being right or wrong; rather it is more of their inability to address issues that are not necessarily of a spiritual nature.

The dilemma that churches face is not unique to any one particular denomination and is certainly much bigger than any one individual's personal experience. What we are facing in the church today is a global state of affairs. And if anything, this reflection has caused me to critically examine the church's current religious practices. compared to those back in the day.

I have discovered that for the most part, some improvement has been made. Bishop T.D. Jakes has certainly championed the case for abused and hurting men, women, and children. Others have established outreach centers, counseling programs, prison rehabilitation efforts, etc. However, even if we go door-to-door, sing a few songs, say a few prayers, and leave assuming that we have touched lives, we are sadly mistaken. The operative word is assume.

When blind Bartimaeus cried out to Jesus in St. Mark, Chapter 10:46-51, the Bible says that Jesus stood still. Then Jesus asked him, "What wilt thou that I should do unto thee?" Bartimaeus answered that he wanted to receive his sight. We know that Jesus healed him and he did, indeed, receive his sight.

My point? I have several:

- Man is triune (spirit, soul, and body). Unless we address all three components, we are not being holistic in our approach and we are not ministering to the total man.

- Jesus did not begin bombarding the man—Jesus stood still. Now days, we are so anxious to give our "spiel" that we make the mistake of overwhelming people with tracts, facts, songs, prayers, scriptures, and personal testimonies.

- Jesus asked Bartimaeus, "What is it that you want?" Do we ever ask first what the immediate needs are? Or do we assume that we know exactly what people need? Do we even allow people to express themselves at all?

I know we mean well, but we cannot begin to know the source of their struggle even if we assume that we can relate just because we came off the streets ourselves; the struggles might be similar, but we are unique individuals—we are not one size fits all. My main point is that we do not need to talk more; we need to talk less, stand still, ask people what it is that they need, and then listen before we respond to our own assumptions.

Then, there is the other extreme where some Christians seem very uncomfortable in the presence of someone straight off the streets. Many churches do not readily embrace or encourage addicts, ex-cons, prostitutes, alcoholics or homosexuals to attend church. And if people in this population wander in, they are required to act soberly and behave or they may be escorted to a remote area of the church by security.

Under layers and layers of being exposed to religious dogma, we have become judgmental, arrogant, and intolerant of people who behave differently than us. We must develop the ability to remain connected to our religious and spiritual tradition, but to approach it critically. While maintaining practices that are, most importantly, biblically based, we must also reject those that do not meet biblical criteria.

So, what is the answer? I believe the search for the answer must begin with us as Christians realizing that not every issue can be resolved through one visit at the altar. Forgiveness and salvation are instant, but Sanctification is a process—not an event. Also, due to the nature of some of the struggles that people come in with from off the streets, they are seldom, truly accepted. That is why some people leave the church and we never see them again.

We must reach them where they are, compel them to come back, and ask them to give us church folk another opportunity to demonstrate and convey the true nature of Christ. And in the words of Bryan Duncan,

> "We all must remember, it's still
> God's Grace we ALL need."

We All Need reprinted by permission

Charles T.Barth and Bryan Duncan Rovi Music 1997

CHAPTER TEN

TOUCHING THE LEPER

Deborah Latchison-Mason

"And He preached in their synagogues throughout all Galilee, and cast out devils. And there came a leper to Him, imploring Him, kneeling down to Him and saying, 'If You are willing, You can make me clean.' Then Jesus, moved with compassion, stretched out His hand and touched him, and said to him, 'I am willing; be cleansed.' As soon as He had spoken, immediately the leprosy left him, and he was cleansed. "

(Mark I:39-42)

In all my studies, I have never read where Jesus passed by a group of sick people without so much as offering to serve them. Sometimes He simply asked, "What do you want me to do?" Consider the case of a leper who approached Jesus with the desperate plea: "If you just want to, you can make me clean." The Bible states that Jesus was moved with pity, reached out and touched the leper saying, "I want to. Be made clean." The man was instantly healed.

Jesus spoke healing in many cases, but when He healed the leper in the first chapter of the book of

Mark, Jesus did the unthinkable by actually touching the man. According to the ethos of that day, lepers were not to be touched. Laws prohibited any kind of contact with lepers, and were strictly enforced. One man—Jesus—was willing to cross all barriers and touch the outcasts of His society.

Note that Jesus did not heal the leper reluctantly or grudgingly but out of genuine compassion. Imagine that you were a leper. How would you feel if you were cured instantly and painlessly of a dreaded illness that progressively had disfigured your body and made you an outcast from society? Jesus dared to touch the 'untouchable' leper. Can the Church do less, and call ourselves His followers?

Jesus' compassion was expressed in ministry. As the Lord saw the needs of suffering people around Him, needs that sparked His emotions, Jesus did not stand idly by. Rather, He engaged in action to alleviate the pain and suffering of the people, and ministered to their needs. Jesus taught over and over again that we should reach out to the sick and offer help and compassion to those in need: "For I was hungry and you gave me food, I was sick, and you took care of me" (Matthew 25:35-36) and "I demand that you love one another" (John 15:12).

Lepers were the untouchables during Jesus' time, but let me identify whom I perceive to be the untouchables of this current day: individuals who have contracted HIV (human immunodeficiency virus), which is the disease that causes AIDS, and individuals with full-blown AIDS (acquired immunodeficiency syndrome). This disease is a plague of monumental proportions worldwide, and is no longer confined only to the original population of gay men. The lives of children, women, heterosexuals, unborn babies, Christians, and non-Christians alike, have been claimed by HIV and AIDS.

Like leprosy, the debilitating disease of HIV/AIDS erects an impenetrable wall between the afflicted and the society of the healthy. On a national level, according to August 2009 stats issued by the CDC (Centers for Disease Control), the HIV/AIDS crisis in America is far from over. Latest estimates suggest that more than 56,000 Americans become infected each year—one person every 9½ minutes—and that more than 1.2 million people in this country are now living with HIV, and approximately 1.1 million people are living with AIDS. Far too many Americans remain at risk for HIV/AIDS, especially African Americans, Latinos, and gay and bisexual men of all races. HIV is the leading cause of death for African

American women ages 25-34. The CDC estimates that roughly 1 in 5 people infected with HIV in the United States is unaware of his or her infection and may be unknowingly transmitting the virus to others. 1

I personally believe that there is no better place for HIV/AIDS victims to be healed physically, emotionally, and spiritually than the Church. It has the influence, the authority, and the capacity to embrace disenfranchised individuals in a community of faith, hope, love and healing. However, the Church is usually the last group of people to respond effectively to vital issues. But not knowing what to do can no longer be used as an excuse. As Christ's followers we must emulate the example He left us by ministering to (touching) those society deems untouchable.

Lecturing on the topic of HIV/AIDS infections for a period of time, however, I have noted that there are four major barriers that hinder ministry in the midst of this pandemic: fear, ignorance, the perception that AIDS is a 'sinner's disease', and the terminal nature of the disease. As Christians, however, we are called to overcome these barriers for the sake of the suffering. Only by confronting stigma and discrimination will the fight against HIV/AIDS be won. As Christians we have a duty to be aggressive learners in this arena and explicit teachers about the nature and causes of this disease.

C-O-M-P-A-S-S-I-O-N, which means literally "to suffer with", should be our chief ministerial response to the AIDS crisis. A first step towards effective healing is taken when we come to understand more completely the divine nature of the compassion we are called to emulate.

Divine compassion calls for divine action. The willingness of Jesus to touch those to whom He ministered becomes even more significant when one remembers that actual, physical contact was not necessary for Jesus to heal. He had the power to cure the sick without even the least amount of physical contact, or physical presence. It is truly powerful when we realize that Jesus chose to touch the leper, the untouchable. Yes, Christ was well aware of the social mores, laws and edicts of His day concerning lepers. But He chose to dismiss the narrow concerns of the masses to embrace with divine intimacy, this poor, hapless soul that all the world determined to be untouchable. And this one act demonstrates His great compassion the most: Jesus did not view this man as untouchable—even though he had leprosy. And it is upon this divine action that the Christian's response to AIDS should be formulated.

Jesus performed many miracles and these miracles were intertwined with His message of God's love for humanity. Such powerful works were central to Jesus' claim that he was the Son of God, the promised Messiah. The Gospel accounts refer to some 35 miracles of Jesus, but the total number of His miracles is not revealed. Matthew 14:14 states, "He [Jesus] saw a great crowd; and he felt compassion for them, and he cured their sick ones."

Have you ever tried shaking hands with a doctor? You go into surgery, you say hello and you go to shake hands and they will sometimes look visibly disturbed. Or you're in a hospital bed and a group of doctors come around, looking quizzical and very peculiar at you. They stand at the bottom of the bed with all of their notes and you go to shake hands and... Do you see the picture?

There is often around the doctor some invisible, imaginary boundary which you must not cross. It is not so much their personal body space as a social exclusion zone. Doctors like to use 'power language'. They use words which you don't understand; they wear funny clothes like bow ties. It is all about setting themselves apart from the perceived riffraff, part of the complex of superiority.

This is true in many professions, not just doctors. For instance, clergymen—yeah, I went there— religious professionals, can often be quite *stuck up* too! This sometimes increases with elevation up the ecclesiastical ladder but not always so. Sometimes even quite ordinary clergy can get a real buzz from saying things like "I won't baptize your baby", or "No I won't marry you'" or "Of course you can't have communion, you're not qualified." This can be said also of laymen and church-going folks period, that we exude an air of being *holier -than-thou*, just like the Pharisees and Sadducees standing around at the time Jesus healed the leper.

Now at the time of Jesus, the religious people (the priests) had combined into their role that of a doctor and a religious leader. Imagine how elevated that would have made them feel. If you had a skin disease you were taken before the priest, and then you had to be pronounced clean by the priest before you could ever return to your role in society. However, you could be sent into exclusion immediately. (Heaven forbid— some poor teenager with a bad case of acne might risk being suddenly cast into outer darkness!)

Listen to these words from Leviticus Chapter 13: The LORD said to Moses and Aaron, "When anyone has a swelling or a rash or a bright spot on his skin that may become an infectious skin disease, he must be brought to Aaron the priest or to one of his sons who is a priest. The priest is to examine the sore on his skin, and if the hair in the sore has turned white and the sore appears to be more than skin deep, it is an infectious skin disease. When the priest examines him, he shall pronounce him ceremonially unclean."

If you were unfortunate to have a bad skin infection then the consequences were severe; the person with such an infectious disease must wear torn clothes, let his hair be unkempt, cover the lower part of his face and cry out, 'Unclean! Unclean!' As long as he has the infection he remains unclean. He must live alone; he must live outside the camp.

One very important thing set Christ apart from the religious leaders of his day: His willingness to touch people. It was that humanity and His readiness to break down the dividing line that banished the leper of His day from society that we must draw upon to respond to the modern-day lepers amongst us.

Much like that leper in the book of Mark, the sufferer from AIDS today craves to be touched. Often it is just a touch which is so important. And so today in this story Jesus touches somebody in the same way and makes it known that he cares and is not worried about catching something.

Leprosy in the time of Jesus was not just a dreaded health problem. It was also a dreaded social disease *and* spiritual disease. The affliction we now call Hanson's disease was not only fearsome in itself. It was also considered to be a curse from God. The consequences were far more deadly than just being physical. Besides having to look forward to years of suffering and disfigurement as well as an early death, lepers were ostracized from the community by Jewish law.

Have you ever seen Michael Jackson's video, *Thriller*, where all the dancers come out of their graves wearing tattered clothes? They are meant to represent the living dead. Lepers would have looked a lot like that, the living dead.

The Jews believed that God himself had laid down the harsh conditions of a leper's lot. They had to wear tattered clothes and let their hair go uncombed and uncut. When meeting any normal or healthy person they had to cover their mouths with a hand and shout out a warning of their own "unclean" condition. In the event that a person was cured and they experienced a remission of the disease, they still had to submit to a ritual cleansing and purging of sin before they would be accepted back into society.

Lepers were not only considered physically loathsome, but they were spiritually loathsome as well. They were physically the living dead, but they were the spiritually dead also. Because so few went into remission or were cured, they were all considered particularly dreadful and persistent sinners.

It is hard for us to imagine the psychological state of such people—husbands, wives, fathers, mothers, children—snatched from their families and forced to fend for themselves among the rocks of the ravine and amidst all the human and non-human terrors that lurked there.

Husbands, fathers, young lovers, would suddenly become pariahs because the religious mentality of the time said that only terrible sinners would be afflicted with such a disease. The point is that a leper had no right to expect either medical care or the embrace of a loving community. Such sinners were beyond God's embrace, per the religious leaders of that time (but it rings so familiar, doesn't it?).

Jesus must have been revolted by the whole notion. But he acts, characteristically, in a way that subverts the prevailing mentality. Rather than being disgusted and even terrified at the request of the leper for assistance, he does not hesitate, indeed, even stresses his determination to do what no one else would have believed possible—to pronounce not only a physical cure for the man when he touches him, but a spiritual cure as well.

In touching the man, Jesus is breaking the moral and religious taboos about lepers and openly, publicly welcoming the man back into human community. So, when he finally orders the man to go and show himself to the priest, it is highly unlikely that Jesus is doing this in order to observe the sanctioned ritual that was required for such persons. It is more likely that Jesus is challenging the religious authorities and his peers to see that God's healing Grace is available to anyone who asks!

The beautiful message here is this; we are forgiven— every last one of us. God's love is there, waiting for us, at all times in our life. It doesn't matter how bad we are, how many mistakes we've made, how horrendously we have fouled up our lives, or the mess we have made of our relationships. The forgiveness is there. We don't have to persuade God to forgive us. We don't have to go through some elaborate ritual or religious exercise to get God to forgive us. The healing which Jesus represents is pure *gift*. That means not earned, not merited, and not won by petition, sacrifice or a good life. According to Jesus, what we need most is available just as quickly, just as easily, just as impacting as Jesus' decisive, compassionate response to the leper—reaching out and making him clean.

Compassion is crucial for genuine ministry, even though this emotion is not readily present, nor easily developed in current society. In fact, total compassion is beyond the realm of human capacity to produce. True compassion is a divine trait and is present in the world only as the fruit of Holy Spirit is manifested in the lives of believers.

A persistent theme in the Bible is the presentation of God as the *Compassionate One.* According to Christian theology, compassion's source lies in the more fundamental emotion of love; love that is agape; whereby persons give of themselves unconditionally for the sake of others. Such love is seldom found in our world today—not even in the Church. However, a perfect example of this emotion can be found always in the compassionate love of God.

His love is not arbitrary; it is not performance-based. For this reason, Christians look at the life of Jesus Christ for divine revelation into the character of God. It is then we discover the loving, compassionate nature of God, and as we come to understand the love of God, the Holy Spirit is able to create in us the kind of compassionate nature that is vital for ministry in the midst of crisis... and the AIDS epidemic is crisis.

The compassionate nature of God as revealed through Jesus Christ, places a great responsibility on Christ's church to be emulators of the compassionate love. His example of selfless love calls us to reflect on the divine character of God daily, without exception or reservation. As believers, the question we should act upon in order to respond with love and compassion to the needs of the suffering is "What *Did* Jesus Do?" The clear, unequivocal answer: He showed compassion to ALL. As Christians, we are commissioned to minister, to touch those in need, never deeming anyone as untouchable—including individuals struggling with AIDS.

Christians should respond to people who have HIV/AIDS in a positive way. This means that we should respond with awareness, love and compassion—not prejudice, denial and apathy. Proverbs 15:28 reads, "The heart of the righteous weighs its answers, but the mouth of the wicked gushes evil."

Christians need to challenge the negative, judgmental, un-Christ like attitudes that still exist toward people with HIV/AIDS. This means that we talk about HIV and AIDS in church and that we work for social change in this area and for an end to the stigma associated with the disease.

As Christ's followers, we should seek to banish fear and misconceptions about HIV and AIDS by providing accurate information about HIV and AIDS. Educational programs for people of all ages are important, but youth deserve comprehensive and open discussion about sex and sexuality. Knowledge is power. *Ignorance kills!*

Churches should be in a position to provide practical and pastoral support for people living with AIDS and their families. There are many ways that churches can become involved, such as; opening the doors of the church for HIV related community meetings, support groups, etc.; providing meals and transportation; or partnering with an AIDS organization in the community to better serve people living with the disease.

Christians need to engage in prayerful dialogue with other churches and faith communities to address this issue from a biblical and godly (not judgmental...) perspective. When we put aside our denominational differences Christians can become a powerful force for change. It is possible to work together.

Finally, to effectively touch the untouchable, our task must begin with a prayerful and conscious effort to be responsive to the presence and working of the Holy Spirit in our lives and in our churches. For the sake of suffering humanity, we must rise to the challenge and be in the earth the loving, serving, compassionate people of God—to the glory of God!

* *FAST FACT #1:* HIV (human immunodeficiency virus) is the disease that causes AIDS (acquired immune deficiency syndrome). A person who is infected with HIV does not automatically attain to AIDS status. AIDS is a deadly condition that develops if HIV is left untreated. However, studies have shown that more people have died while yet in HIV status than have died with a diagnosis of full-blown AIDS. As stated earlier, HIV is the leading cause of death of African-American women aged 25-34.

FAST FACT #2:   Key Snapshot of the U.S. Epidemic Today (The Kaiser Family Foundation, "The HIV/AIDS Epidemic in the United States", October 2011 Fact Sheet)

- Number of new HIV infections, 2009: 54,100
- Number of people living with HIV/AIDS in America: 1.2 million and 1.1 million respectively.
- Number of AIDS deaths in the United States since beginning of epidemic: 617,025, including more than 16,000 in 2008.
- Percent of people infected with HIV but are unaware of it: 20%.

FAST FACT #3:   Estimates of new HIV infections were increased by the Centers for Disease Control and Prevention (CDC), and indicate that there were approximately 50,000 people newly infected with HIV per year between 2006 and 2009. New infections, however, continue at far too high a level, with an estimated real-average of 56,300 Americans becoming infected with HIV each year.

FAST FACT #4: From 2002 through the end of 2008, an estimated 240,627 blacks with an AIDS diagnosis had died in the United States (Centers for Disease Control, Surveillance Report).

FAST FACT #5: The WHO (World Health Organization) released a report in November 2009 that stated (1) an estimated 33.4 million people worldwide are living with HIV/AIDS, (2) there are some 2.7 million new infections worldwide each year, and (3) HIV/AIDS is the leading cause of death among young women of reproductive age, globally.

FAST FACT #6: Alarming Trends - Every six and a half seconds, another person is infected with HIV. Every 10 seconds, one person dies of an AIDS-related illness. There are an estimated 11,200 new HIV infections and nearly 8,000 deaths worldwide every day (XVI International AIDS Conference).

BUT...

*F*AST *F*ACT *#7:*   He [Jesus] was wounded for our transgression; he was bruised for our iniquity: the chastisement of our peace was upon him; and with his stripes, we are HEALED (Isaiah 53:5 KJV).

PART

THE
CALLED

CHAPTER ELEVEN

FROM GANGS TO GLORY

Joe "San Joe" Whitson

IN THE BEGINNING

My mother was raped and conceived me; I was that child that just about everybody except my mother wanted to abort. She was fifteen when she got raped and sixteen when she had me. Needless to say the situation was not ideal, and the fact that my mother dropped out of school in sixth grade made matters even worse. Addiction put a strain on my mother to the point; a life of crime was nearly inevitable.

One of my earliest memories was of my brother's father (he has since changed in many regards) beating my mother bloody. I was five years old. I didn't know what to do, so I reacted. I grabbed the butcher knife, climbed up on the bed behind him, and then raised the knife with both hands above my head, in preparation to drive it into his back. At which point my mother screamed (had she not screamed I may not be writing this story today). He turned and took the knife from me. Then I told him in tears "when I get bigger I am going to kill you."

We moved shortly after that from Las Vegas to California. This is where I first noticed my mother's heroin addiction had spiraled out of control. I hated the people that brought drugs to the house because my mother would get high and not be able to spend any time with us (you see the heroin would just leave her in a daze, trying to keep her head up, nodding in and out of consciousness).

My tio (uncle) Tomas was a great guy always ready to play with us, he wasn't my real uncle, but I loved him as much if not more than my real uncles. He was a tough guy biker type that people didn't mess with. I often wonder how I didn't make the connection that he was part of the problem. Well one day he came up missing hours led to days and we were all really worried.

Well my mom went to his sister's house, to cop some dope, and Tomas's niece kept telling my mom come look at my new doll tia (aunt). At first my mother said, "no not right now mija (beloved or loved one)," then my mom finally went with the young lady. To her surprise the little girl brought her to the closet and there was tio Tomas foaming at the mouth shaking. My mom got out of there in a hurry, next I heard that they were nowhere to be found and someone had dropped Tomas's body in an alley. He was stuck in a coma for years.

The drama was too thick so we moved to the Bay area. My mother was excited because this is where she had grown up. Her addiction got worse; I remember the many times people were overdosing at the hotel or house we were staying at. I remember one time we were at a hotel and this lady wanted some dope; my mother was reluctant to share, citing the fact that she thought the lady couldn't handle the cut of dope my mother had. So they all get high and sure enough the lady overdosed. They rushed her to the tub. I remember them running up and down the stairs. You know the kind at the old hotels with the metal support running down the middle and the cement stairs, with the rocks on the top of each stair for traction. And when you run up and down them they make that weird sound. Well they ran up and down getting buckets of ice trying to fill the tub with ice, but they forgot to shut the door all the way. So my brother and I sat and watched them slap the lady, until she came back to life. Another time my Tio Doug (not my real tio) fell out (overdosed), this time my mother had the door shut, but the window in her room was open. So the whole neighborhood heard her yelling, slapping him and calling him all sorts of names, the nicest one being *pooh butt.*

TEEN YEARS

This was my life growing up and I hated the fact, but there was nothing I could do to change it. Eventually it wore me down. I started drinking early, but didn't start smoking weed and cigarettes until I was about fourteen years old. As my habits changed, so did my friends. By fifteen I was experimenting with PCP and acid. I got jumped into my hood. They took me outside and jumped me for five minutes, but I did pretty good so when I got inside the other homies said it didn't look like I even got jumped so they took me outside for three more minutes.

We were very violent young men, a band of thieves, greedy, prideful, thought we knew it all and you couldn't tell us nothing. People got robbed, stabbed, run over, beat up and shot and most times we didn't have a good reason; yet we were convinced in our own minds that what we were doing was helping our people. Actually we were holding our communities hostage, making huge contributions to the destabilizing of those communities, shaping the minds of those coming behind us to do the same or worse, holding them hostage to their pride or male role belief system (unknowingly at the time), and terrorizing them in the process.

Next I got locked up a couple times for fighting, once on a weapons charge, and for being with people who also were on probation. I meet my probation officer, he came into the conference room before court. I thought he was a pimp; he was wearing a bright purple suit and he talked and walked like one too. When he says to me, "So Ira Joe Angel Whitson" I react and I say to him, "You got the wrong room, homie." So he says "Oh" and leaves. Then he comes back a few minutes later laughing and says "Oh you think you're funny." So I get mad and tell him, "I told you homie you got the wrong room."

So he goes and talks to my grandmother and she explains to him that I didn't know my real name, and that I had been going to school under an alias, Joe Gonzalez, since the third grade and Joe Hernandez before that. So after he checks it all out (school records) he comes back and we talk. But the crucial mistake he made was filing my paperwork under Joe Gonzalez.

In Juvenile hall I was fighting a lot so they decided to teach me a lesson and send me to the ranch. At the ranch I got in a fight and split another boy's forehead open. So they sent me back on new charges. I had lawyer's that were from school (part of their interning, I think) so they were trying to win and it looked good. But then my probation officer dropped the charges, looking to re-file them because he knew that I was going to beat it (he was a very prideful man). He even told my lawyers to beware of a courtroom surprise. So my lawyers asked the judge to drop them with prejudice to re-filing but the judge denied it. So they came up with new charges terrorist threats (which I didn't do), defacing county property (which I did do, scraped my hood in the cement in my cell two or three feet tall above the window with a piece of my shoe). It worked out to twenty years, because they said I was trying to kill a guy who switched gangs. I wasn't even in on it, but a guy from my gang said that I threatened him even though I didn't even send him a message to do anything to him. I think someone just used my name to scare him. So I tried everything. Glen Allen hills in Pennsylvania wouldn't accept me, Vision Quest in Arizona wouldn't accept me, even ROP wouldn't accept me. So I took the plea bargain for a program at the ranch understanding it was my last chance and they were looking to get me next time. But the fact my probation officer would use someone from my hood and make up charges and drop and re-file the case that I could not have good counsel, made me lose what little faith I had in the justice system.

ON THE RUN

I felt played like I couldn't get any justice, so I ran from the ranch. I was running with some other guys, but once we got out the gate, the staff jumped in a car trying to catch us, so we hid in the tall grass. But they were driving through the tall grass really fast and almost ran a couple of us over.. I got separated from the other guys and the car was on me, so I hit a fence and one of the staff followed. It was almost like a cartoon; one minute the staff is chasing me, then I slow down because I see a whole herd of steers taller than I was. We look at each other and I yell "bulls!" So now I am chasing him and the bulls are chasing us! He gets over the fence and thinks I am going that way. The car is there waiting and they think they got me. But at the last minute I turn and run along the fence to another fence dive through the barbed wire (cut my face a little bit in the process), but I got away. I found a half empty aqueduct and ran through that, ducking so no one could see me. I was up to my waist in whatever was in that aqueduct (it stunk) and I got thorns all in my pants from running through the tall grass. And I am running full speed for like thirty or forty minutes, when my legs start cramping up from running so much. I am literally in the tall grass trying to stretch out my legs in tears because it felt like my muscles were tearing apart in several different places. But I forgot that the night I ran was Blvd Nights, so no one was home on the east side; they were cruising and I was staying in the north side at the time, so I couldn't go there.

So I decided to go to Santa Clara the police would not look for me there, the only problem was it was fifteen to twenty more miles. I got to Santa Clara High in the morning hoping to catch one of my homies. Luckily some of their old ladies recognized me and took me home to shower up. I called my grandma she got me some clothes and some money. So we got some twenty-four packs and celebrated. I caught up with my other homies from San Jose a couple days later. This is when I formally got introduced to speed. The Speed stole my mind; I was lost and couldn't grasp reality. I was out committing worse crimes than ever before running with shadier characters than ever before and the results were worse than ever before. I can honestly say I was on the fast track to addiction, prison, heart-ache and death.

It got too hot in San Jose, so I went to Reno, got an ID under Ira Joe Whitson and hid, but I didn't change how I thought, so I decided to leave for Lake Havasu City, Arizona

ARIZONA

In Arizona the first time I was out partying. We broke into a few cars, stole a camcorder, laptop and a few other items and try to sell them. The guy who broke in the cars with me told me he had a buyer, his uncle. I was okay with this. When the uncle gets there I ask him if he is a cop, he says "no", so I sell him the merchandise. Twenty minutes later the police are raiding; they can't get me on the floor so they bring in my aunt, who I was staying with, at gunpoint telling me to get down. She is scared and I am out my mind (this furthered my hatred of police—to see them use an innocent woman in that way). So I get on the ground. They take me in book me and I am thinking it's nothing. They get me in court I am smiling thinking I'll be out in no time. The judge reads off the charges and I am nonchalant until he says "Twenty-eight years. How do you plead?" It literally took my breath away, I was thinking to myself, Wow, I didn't even do nothing! But the laws in Arizona were different than in California.

I fought the case for a year, finally my young partner who was with me took the wrap, saying he did it all, so all they had on me is the sale. I get a plea bargain for three years' probation and a year in the county, they even eventually suspended the year in the county.

So I got a job at Payless Shoes and met Jim Grey, the manager. He was a Christian and starts ministering to me. Since I like to know what I am talking about, I start reading the Bible so I can hold a conversation with him. He eventually has to let me go, but he sowed a seed in my life.

After that I was still living so foul. Some of my enemies banded together and caught me slipping and beat me with guns and I swear, if the young man with the ice pick knew what he was doing I would be dead! I am very thankful that he was scared. So, full of pride, I came back and struck on them as well. Afterward their leader and I thought it best to squash the problem, because we both knew the next step would end with people dying. But they wanted to make sure. So they had a guy I knew, one I didn't know was with them, get me to an old truck with a guy I didn't know. He was saying, "They stabbed you; they stabbed me too. Let's go get them". I was like, "I can't, we squashed. It's over," But he kept pressing me, "We can go get them", so I responded, "I'd be a punk if I went and got them after I told them it was squashed." But he kept saying "They stabbed you. Don't you want to get them?" So finally I got mad and said, "Look I told you, me and Louie squashed it, but if you got a problem with Louie then handle your business, but I tell you this; you better come hard, because Louie ain't no punk." I jumped out of the truck . The guys outside the truck were surprised to see me get out alive. I didn't realize it 'til right then: it was a set up with guys in all four directions as look outs. All the stores were closed with no cars, only the truck. I was slipping and they could've killed me. I truly believe it was the Lord who kept me alive.

About that time I met my future wife and we started dating, and it is a wonderful time in my life. She taught me what love is and how to love; and for that I am eternally grateful. A couple years later she signed up for a Bible college. A guy called her back and I answered, we started talking and both felt as if we knew each other. And as we kept talking I realized it was Jim. So we talked and I had just written my first Christian song called "What I Believe." I read it to him and he said, "It lines up." I started going to his church and loved God; but I was blind to my own sin.

SALVATION AND MINISTRY

Months later I was in the back of the church, just listening. I don't even remember what Jim was preaching. Then all of a sudden I was in a different place—it was more vivid than a Pixar movie—and I see the Lord on the cross. He didn't say anything, just took a breath and breathed His last. At that point it all became clear and I understood. I tried to wipe away the tears, but I couldn't... *Niagara Falls.*

Years later we ministered to the kids in South Stockton at the park but they were not receiving our witness. I saw a guy who's head was cracked like an egg (scars) 1/4 inch gashes all over the front. I looked to a brother and said "The guy who did that probably don't even care that he did that." At the end of the event we started cleaning up and we were also passing out flyers for the next event. I go up to the guy with the scars and invite him; he starts hitting himself in the head and pointing at me. I couldn't understand what he was saying, because he had lost the ability to properly speak by whoever did that to him." So I am asking him questions, "San Jose?" He shakes his head yes and I am tripping—it can't be, so I ask "The West Side?" He shakes his head yes. I say "Vine and Virginia?" He said yes and both his hands were on me and I looked down and it was like de ja vu.

When I saw the rosary bead tattoo on his hand, I knew it was the same as the guy I beat with a piece of sidewalk in a gang fight when we were surrounded on enemy turf doing a *check stroll.* I beat him until he was foaming out his mouth and his head. I remember his hand because he was holding on to my shirt for his life. My Ben Davis shirt ripped from the armpit to the bottom with his blood all over it. I remember his hand because I was trying to beat him off of me and he was holding on.

The memory hit me so hard when I looked at him again; I fell on my knees and started weeping, asking for his forgiveness because I had done this to him. Then he pointed—he pointed at me, pointed at himself, and pointed up towards heaven. It broke me. Then the kids who had not received our witness came over and asked, "What... you did that to him?" See it wasn't real when we were just talking about it but when a victim of ours was a guy that lived among them they could no longer deny it. So we ministered to them all and they all prayed a prayer of salvation with us. I do not know if they all believed it in their hearts but I *know* God moved that day.

A few months later I was ministering in Lake Havasu City, The pastor had told me that some guys that knew me were coming and they were trying to get out the gang-life. I praise God. I was doing a sound check and I saw some gang members come in bald headed, tattoos all over the head so I walked over to minister to them and share a testimony.

I walk over to them and say, "Hey guys I am San Joe and I been through a few things that you might be going through or have already been through and I would like to tell you how I got free." And the main one goes "Joe, it's Johnny," I was like "cool, but let me tell you about my life." And he says, "Joe, I don't think you understand *it's Johnny*,". And he was right, I didn't recognize who he was. So he continued "Joe, it's Johnny, it's Payaso. "Right then my flesh rolled up my back and I was the *old man*. I have never had it happen like before or since.

I try to get close to him because I remember when he and his brother beat me over the head with river rocks until I was a mess. See in Lake Havasu City it is so hot that grass hardly grows, so people decorate their yards with river rock (and this was the décor of their apartments). I fought for as long as I could 'til I fell out. I got up; got in the car and bounced to the hospital. Police pulled us over; I knew if they told, I couldn't get my revenge, so I told them just to say they picked me up at the spot all bloody and I told them I got hit by a car. So it took them out of the equation.

And here I am in front of him finally all in my flesh, and he is saying "Joe it would have never have happened if you didn't come to the house." This only made me madder because I went there, to get my wife's sixteen year old cousin out of there. At this point I am like a ravenous wolf stalking his prey, getting closer and he is stepping back saying "I'm sorry it would never have happened—*spensa homie.*" Then Sister Darlene came over and was like "San Joe are you okay?" and I was like, "Yeah, don't worry, just go," but she knew something was wrong, so she persisted and kept asking. Then I see in my head, the guy I thought I killed and remember how he forgave me. So the pressure dropped from me and I was calm and knew I had to forgive him. So he kept going asking forgiveness and I forgave him. But then he switched, talking about being in the Pen and how they got him with a razor a couple times, but everyone who got him with a razor caught a pick (a long shank.) So I turn to him and say, "Don't you know you can die in the church." He begins to panic and his brother sits down says, "Joe you won't do nothing in the church will you? I don't even bang no more." But what I meant was going to church cannot save your soul, only relationship with Christ and being born again.

But I did not get a chance to share that message they called me back up to finish my sound check, so I rushed it, then rushed outside and caught them. I said, "Hey don't leave," I was tripping. I explained what I meant but they didn't believe me; I could see it in their eyes. They promised to come back later but never did.

So I learned a hard lesson that day; the flesh can get in the way, if you let it, in ministry, but if you move out of the way and let God have His way He can do amazing things through you.

I didn't understand at that time, but I learned that the flesh has to die from that experience. Killing it was the hard part. I started prison ministry in 2004 I remember praying, going through the gates the first time, "Lord if it's your will I am going to minister to these kids, but if not I guess I'll be ministering in the county." Ever since that day the Lord has blessed me to see lives of young men changed because their hearts were turned to the Lord. Even the ones who have doubted the most can't deny, that the Lord has changed me and that He can change them. In 2005 I injured my back and was bed rest for two years but that didn't stop me from going out and ministering in the Department of Juvenile justice That's when I believe I won over those who didn't believe when they saw how much I loved them; in spite of my obvious pain I still drove those miles and came and ministered to the young men.

I went from ministering once in a while to every fifth Sunday, and then once a month on Thursday night in Chad, once a month Sunday in OH Close ,and eventually every Thursday in Preston.

Now I do every second Sunday in OH Close and every fifth Sunday in Chad. I have seen countless testimonies of lives changed, not only produced while in prison, but also that are still being manifest to this day, after they have been released. All I can do is thank God for allowing me to be a part of their transformation.

In 2007 I also started Bible College, which was a great experience. It helped me to grow and learn God's word more than I ever have. It taught me how to study and that knowing God is so important

In 2007 Project Impact hired me as a facilitator. I have worked in Paso Robles (Closed in 2007), Dewitt Nelson (Closed in 2008), Preston (Closed in 2010), OH Close (since 2008) and Chaderjian (since 2008). I have built relationships through Prison ministry and IMPACT that have brought down so many walls in these young people's lives. It is a blessing to be used by the Lord.

I started 1 day a week in 2007 at Paso Robles until the close of Paso Robles. Then I went to 4-5 days a week in 2007 (Dewitt Nelson, Oh Close, Chaderjian and Preston) until the close of Dewitt Nelson in 2008. Then it was consistently 5 days a week (Chaderjian, OH Close and Preston) until the close of Preston in 2010. And currently work 5 days a week in OH Close and Chaderjian. It been a tremendous blessing to work at the DJJ. It has helped in my prison ministry, because it has opened the door for some that might not otherwise attend to chapel to come, just because I was teaching that Sunday. Not only that, but I get to show the young men I care and that opens the door for additional ministry.

KEYS TO EVANGELISM

I. PREPARATION

- Praying: You must seek the Lord for the direction (who to speak to, when to speak, how to speak, et cetera) it may or may not be the direction you want to go, but Gods will is perfect. (Ephesians 6:18, Jude 1:20-21, Romans 12:11-13, Philippians 4:6-7)
- Fasting: Sometimes in seeking the Lord we may want to fast, to show God just how serious we are, about hearing His voice, seeking His will, or fasting for intercession on behalf of a brother or sister in Christ

and unbelievers. (Proper Fasting Isaiah 58)

- Studying: It is important to know your Bible and stay in the Word, you never know what questions may arise. (2 Timothy 2:15, 2 Timothy 4:1-5, 1 Peter 3:15,1 Peter 5:2)

II. MINISTERING

- Be bold: Know that if the Lord led you to speak, then "His Will" will go forth. (1 Peter 1:21) this is why it is so important to be led.

- Do not be afraid: Sometimes what they say about us, or how they may look at us or what they may try to do to us, can effect whether or not we do what the Lord is leading. And remember if they reject you, they are not rejecting you, but Him who sent you, you only have to speak. (Ezekiel 2:1-10, Ezekiel 3:4-11, Ezekiel 3:16-21, Exodus 4:11-12).

- Do not make excuses: I am too young, don't know enough, to old, et cetera If God sends you he will empower you for the work. (Jeremiah 1:4-10)S

- Show them you care: If you are not invested, the people will be able to see it. If you are not invested pray for the Lord to put empathy, sympathy, and compassion in your heart. Sometimes just imagining yourself in another's shoes can help.

- Listen to the people. (1 Corinthians 13:1-3) Know your audience: If this is possible this will help you greatly, in trying to reach them. (1 Cor. 9:19-23)

III. AFTERWARD

Intercede: Remember to be praying over those you have ministered to. Pray that the message takes root in their heart, that the Lord will send others to water that seed. Pray for their protection—both spiritually and physically. (1 Corinthians 3:5-15, Ephesians 1:15-17, Phi 1:3-5, 1 Thessalonians 1:2, 1 Timothy 2:1, 2 Tim 1:3-4, Philemon 1:4, Hebrews 5:7)

And last; It is extremely important to know God, to know His voice and follow His lead. Without this key element, everything else you do will be as you see fit or in your own strength. So if you do nothing else, know His voice and follow His lead. I promise that He will always be with you and lead you if you let Him. It will not always be easy, but the more mature you become the heavier the burden He can entrust you with. The heavier the burden, the sweeter the fruit for the kingdom you will produce.

CHAPTER TWELVE

BREAKING THE SILENCE

Heireina "Rein" Johnson

I will never forget the house I grew up in. It was a fairly modest home built on almost the end of a steep hill on Bowdoin Street in San Francisco, CA. 1214 Bowdoin was the exact address. I still get chills when I hear those numbers. It's like I'm being teleported back to its steps and seeing all that I'd much rather forget at times. I remember that house being so meticulously painted—a peachy color, I recall, with chocolate brown trim. I even remember the day we all painted it.

I was responsible for painting the concrete stairs brown, stopping to play painted tic-tac-toe with my brother on occasion. I still have many of the scars from hurting myself on those stairs so often. I can even recall myself sitting on those stairs and looking up at the windows of the other houses.

Being the only girl in the neighborhood I didn't have many friends except for my brother's friends. I learned to jump dirt hills, slide down them on cardboard, and play basketball, but mostly I sat on those stairs and enjoyed the time away from the inside. I often wondered if other families around us lived like us, if other kids had a grandmother who hated and abused them or why my grandmother wasn't anything like those of my playmates who lavished them with gifts, support, and love.

You see my grandmother was my primary care provider during the day. She was a very strong woman by exterior perception who could spark fear into fear itself, but I sensed that inside she was frail, bitter, and deeply wounded. She never talked about her troubles. Instead she was a functional drunk often burying her pain in several full glasses of the alcohol of choice, a cigarette, the soap operas, and B.B. King.

I watched her a lot during these times and most times she was present in body, but not in the spirit or the mind. Her hollow frame occupying her usual spot on the couch everyday was a mere hologram.

All that was truly "alive" in her was the brokenness and sadness that forever lived in her eyes and in her reflection at the bottom of her glass of alcohol.

Sensing a deep and internal battle within her, I made it a personal mission to make her happy, although I was a mere toddler. I learned early that it was best to please her. I painted pictures; I made charms and even wrote songs and poems for her. Many times I stood flat-footed before her, such a little thing, and sang along with her blues records to entertain her. Most of my arts and craft projects were dedicated to her because I wanted her to feel loved. She offered a smile or hug on occasion and even hung this ridiculous wind chime I'd made her in my kindergarten class over her bedroom door. She displayed all the school photos I'd clay framed and kept all the pictures I had drawn, but it was never enough. Her happiness was always so fleeting, and I always received the lion's share of abuse because of it. Nothing I did mattered because when she looked at me she didn't see me. I was her splitting image. The little girl she couldn't bare to look at had escaped from her insides and was staring at her everyday bringing back too many of her own painful memories.

LESS THAN GARBAGE

I'd grown accustomed to the yelling and the fits of rage. I was used to merciless beatings both wet and dry for no apparent reason other than the fact that I existed. I could withstand the verbal abuse and her telling me I was evil like my father and a burden to my mother, usually by pretending she was talking to someone else or by hiding inside my own head, but there was one event that would change my life forever. There was no pretending my way out. There was no place in my head that I could escape to that would ease me out of the pain of this one.

It was a warm day. I was dressed in my Sunday clothes and my hair was dutifully combed, but it wasn't Sunday. My grandmother, my brother, and I boarded a bus headed to an unknown destination. There was an unusual calm and something strange in my grandmother's atmosphere, but I thought it best to remain quiet while I fondled with the ribbon in my hair.

I remember entering a house I'd never been to. It had a strange and musky smell. No plants or art lined the walls as I had been accustomed to, in fact, it didn't seem homey at all. Instead it had sadness and darkness about it, and I didn't want to be there. I immediately longed for my mom because I didn't feel safe. Impending doom was evident to me for some strange reason, and everything in me wanted to turn back and find the safety of outside.

I grabbed my tiny stomach as if scolding the butteries and uncontrollable fear bubbling within. I turned around to seek for the comfort of my grandmother's presence but she was unusually silent and distant. Normally she would have held my hand or instructed me not to touch anything, and to stay close where she could keep a watchful eye on me, but on this day she seemed miles away and only looked straight ahead as someone I didn't know (and had never seen before) walked us down a long corridor that seemed to stretch on for miles.

We reached a room that was dimly lit. There was a very large bed inside for such a small room and a small television was situated on the floor. I was led to sit on the bed by this strange man, and knowing my grandmother would strangle me for disobedience, I did as I was told, but an unfamiliar fear had gripped me. Something was off; something was just plain wrong about this entire scene.

I searched for my grandmother's eyes but they never found mine—not directly. There was a scolding from her peripheral vision that almost dared me to move, but never direct eye contact. It was intentional. I recall the look of indignation and satisfaction on her countenance before I watched her turn her back, walk toward the door, exit, and close it behind her. For the first time in my life, I had come to know what it felt like to be abandoned.

Jarred by the repeatedly opening door, I looked up to see several men entering the room and watched them as they stood over the bed I was on. I was eventually dragged up toward the head of the bed by my left and right arms. I was horrified. I heard pants being unzipped and felt grown men's hands on my tiny person that they shouldn't have been touching. I could do nothing but stare in dreadful silence. I remember my dress being lifted up to my chest, and I wished it had covered my eyes. My legs were cast violently apart, and I wanted to yell for my grandmother, but it had occurred to me that I had been given away. I didn't know the word *prostitution* then, but I remember feeling like garbage discarded and thrown to the dogs.

The breathing was heavy all around me. There wasn't a side that I could turn to that would allow me to avoid their faces or their sounds. There wasn't even wall space that I could focus on that wasn't colored by a stranger standing over me. They laughed above me and took their turns giving me instructions.

I remember searing pain as my eyes focused on a ribbon now strewn on the bed that had once been in my hair. I stared at the ribbon trying to forge a fantasy, but I found no solace in any of my imaginary worlds that day. Nothing could have prepared me or saved me from the feeling of that moment but death itself. I wanted my dad; I wanted to join him in heaven.

I believe it is divine that my memory blacks out here. I cannot recall how that moment in my life ended, and I have no recollection of watching any of those many men leave the room. I don't even remember the long bus ride back home. I cannot recall if I caught my grandmother's eyes when all was said and done, but I do know that I never ever looked her in her eyes again—not even when we visited her in the rest home knowing that was the last day I'd ever see her again alive. I was traumatized.

I cannot tell you when or how I was cleaned, when we left that horrific house, or even how I had arrived back at home. I just remember waking up full of shame and confusion, and that this was the day I became "strange" according to my grandmother, but the word was introvert. That was the day I learned to believe that I was less than garbage. It was the day my mind called me worthless, and my heart and spirit

—broken and shattered—said, "we agree." That was the day that my internal castle turned into a cave

My grandmother wanted to destroy me. I knew that she hated me for her own reasons, I just didn't know to what extent. I wanted partially to applaud her, for she had managed to break through my imaginary barriers and penetrate my internal castle. She defeated my internal army and had managed to work her way past all of my booby traps and barriers, which had so diligently kept her out of my emotional kingdom.

I received many beatings after that day, but they ceased to affect me and yielded little to no tears after that incident in that strange house. There was nothing worse that she could do to me than what she had done that day. She could have given me a thousand lashes after that or burned me, but nothing would've felt any worse. My grandmother had wanted to destroy me, and... she won. I waved my little white flag and decided to believe her when she called me "nothing."

Surely anyone who was worth anything wouldn't have been subjected to that kind of abuse at such a young age; right? Surely no respectable man would take that kind of advantage of such a frail and helpless child if that child were worth anything at all; right? I blamed myself for being so penetrable, and I often wished she had just killed me.

In the short time I had lived, I had never known what hatred was. My grandmother's came like fiery darts through her words and accusations, whippings, abuse, and neglect, but I was hidden away from it all and protected by the walls I had built inside myself.

This newfound hatred overwhelmed and consumed me since that fretful day, so much so, I couldn't find happy. There was no joy in playing with my dolls or escaping to any of my imaginary worlds. The wicked witch was always there, and I was always afraid of her. Although I'd learned to read extraordinarily well at three, the words on the pages refused to come alive to me anymore. I retreated into an internal cave and simply refused to come out and face the world.

Her hatred, which became my own, consumed me so, that my asthmatic condition was frequently aroused at the thought and sight of her. Inside me something terrible was growing and it was adding to my shame by the hour. I sat in my internal caves and I yelled and screamed about how much I hated her until my blood boiled. I hated her until I could see the fear in her eyes when we had to share a bed. I relished in her inability to turn her back to me at night, and I dreamt that the daggers of my indescribable pain would loom over her taunting her and interrupting her pleasantries in her own dreams.

I hated myself, I hated my dad because he was dead, and I hated my mom because she wasn't there to save me and was in no position to get us away from my grandmother. I even hated my own voice because I had been so powerless to use it when it mattered most. Underneath my pretend smile was an emotional load that made me close my throat so as not to let any more words escape. I vowed that I would never speak again. Consumed and overwhelmed with sadness, there were just no words worth speaking. I became a hollow and empty shell to everyone and everything around me... only they didn't notice.

HERO

I must have been eight years old or so, went he walked into my life. He was over six feet tall and was as handsome as the morning sun. He had a coolness about his way that made me smile and a shine and a *swag* that made me understand why he was my mother's "one.'" The way he made her smile made me dance inside; it was something I hadn't felt for a long time. No one else could see it, but I could see how shiny his armor was. Although his sword was invisible, I was sure that he carried one because in his presence I felt safe. He was a tall knight to me and I was his little princess basking in his eternal glow.

I was now something I had always longed to be... a daddy's girl.

I found a love for the imagination again and often plotted secretly his revenge against my grandmother. One day I'd tell him the stories of how she'd abused me, and I'd shine and polish his breastplate and shield before he marched out to avenge me. But, at the moment, spending time with him in the real world was just plain nice. For the time being, my new dad was the barrier that stood between me and all of the hell I had known, and I was satisfied. I started to believe God had heard me. I started to believe my biological father had sent my step-dad in his stead; I just started to believe in something again.

My step-dad proved to be very strict, but it was a small price to pay for the freedom I had come to know. When all my chores were done, I would eagerly jump into his lap and listen to him sing his silly songs. At other times I was mesmerized by his booming laugh at something well beyond my youthful understanding on the television, or I just sat in his presence feeling the comfort of his shadow. He held in his hands my essence and it was unknown to him that he was responsible for my cotton candy dreams and the forging of a new internal fortress wherein I danced under the summer sun, even when it was raining outside. My dad was plain and simply my hero.

When I was close to ten, I began to exchange my youthful and childish dreams for more adult-like understanding. Dolls were now silly and pretend castles were for babies. I was growing now and taking my rightful place in the world. My days in Summer were spent lazily lounging on the porches of my school mates and neighbor's houses chatting about the important things like the latest New Edition song and what we would get for Christmas or what we'd wear on the first day of school. We sucked on icees we had made in Styrofoam cups and ate pickles and quarter candy—usually *Now and Laters* (any flavor).

I'll never forget the day my friend invited me into her home. I felt sorry for her having to live in such an unclean and roach infested environment. She shared stories of her fears, and I would often sneak her something to eat. Hanging at her house became the regular thing to do just to keep her spirits up. In her mind she had no mom, so I gave her the hugs she needed, some of my clothes, and the pats on the back she couldn't get elsewhere. It was sad really.

One day while playing "lookout" as she looked for spare change for icees in her mother's room, I was surveying my surroundings and feeling uncomfortable.

I just knew we would get caught and I'd be *in for it* when I got home. My friend was taking change from her mother's drawers when I noticed something on top of it that sent a vicious chill through me. I couldn't believe what I was seeing. I was confused and I couldn't speak. On her dresser was a picture of my dad.

I didn't know how old it was or where she had gotten if from, but I wondered if it blew up on their doorstep or met her mother in the street and she just happened to keep it; however, no reasoning made me feel better. As we walked back outside, I was quiet. I looked up at the sky and it became suddenly clear to me; the winds were changing. That was the last time I would play with my friend.

BOUND BY SILENCE

At home I began to watch my dad. His armor seemed so faded now. I longed for the cotton candy dreams again and to hear his laughter one more time but he was new to me. He was jumpy and moody, anxious and often unsettled. Our days were filled with his yelling, and I recall and overwhelming sense of gloom. His thoughts often betrayed him; they were almost piercing at times. I saw how much he hated everything around him... including himself. I watched him throw away applications that he struggled to read or fill out. To ease his frustration, I often helped him by reading many of them to him and doing his writing for him.

I remember watching him stomp down the stairs of our small apartment building and out into the streets walking toward my former playmate's house with his brother. I watched with piercing anger as they walked boldly across the street with the big brown paper bags his brother would bring over and the secrecy that hovered over them. I'd become all too familiar with those bags and increasingly more aware of what was in them, though I didn't want to admit it. It didn't take a genius to know that he was addicted to something well beyond my human reach. I refused to let myself really see though; it was too unbearable.

I searched relentlessly for the knight I had come to know. I waited endlessly to recapture his gaze and for the time to remind him of our happiness—to snap him out of this stupor he seemed to be bound to, but he couldn't face me. He could never look me in my eyes. His retinas were blank and empty; they told the story of someone lost in his own cave now.

BROKEN... AGAIN

Much too old now to sit on his lap, I found it somewhat odd that he beckoned to me to do so. I wasn't afraid,

I was just unsure. So many questions were swirling around in my head. I wanted to know why my friend's mom had his picture on her dresser. I wanted him to explain why he had become someone new and distant, and I wanted to shred every paper bag that had ever come across my line of sight. I wanted to tell him that our old castle was beginning to crumble and that I wanted his strong hands to fix it.

I walked over to him silently instead with my tongue pressed against the roof of my mouth and my hands sheepishly in my pockets. The way he grabbed my arm and drew me to him was lifeless and empty of the warmth I had once known. He wasn't mean or unloving, but he was suspicious, and for the first time as I stood that close to him with his breath blowing hot against my cheek, I felt unsafe.

"Sit on my lap," he said in a tone I hadn't known before. It was a suspiciously careful sound as I recall. The lump that was forming in my chest had somehow found its way to my throat and I was sure that any second I was going to *hurl*. Looking back on it, I wish I had. I vaguely remember him asking me if I knew how much he loved me. I gave a soft and insecure, "yes" before I buried myself again in my silence. "When you love someone, you give them massages," he said. The statement sent me back to that room I had been in when I was just a toddler. I wanted to run and escape, but there was nowhere else to go except inside myself.

I had been here before and it had brought me so much shame and hurt. I was so unsure of what was happening, but before I had any chance of contemplating it he had grabbed my hand, forcing me to inappropriate contact with him against my will.

What was I doing? Why couldn't I speak? I wanted to beg him not to do this and to let me run away, but the words were bundled up in my chest fighting with each other. At one point I could swear I had felt them pounding against my lips, but my lips were swollen shut and pursed uncontrollably.

I cannot recall how I got in my room. I just remember looking up and I was there, and I began to cry. I cried for myself as that helpless toddler, I cried for the man my stepfather had become and the one I had lost in him, I cried for being so stupid and so withered under the pressure that I had let this happen to me again, and I cried because I believed it was *my fault* and that I could never tell.

I had come to absolutely hate his voice always calling to me, but deep down I still loved him as my dad... and I hated myself because I did. I had come to know his patterns and routines. It always started with a crook in his neck that he needed me to rub or that walk on his back that he needed me to give.

I hated him—at least that's what I told myself. It always ended the same. To this day, in spite of several attempts at doing more with me, I am amazed he never raped me. Often angry, he would send me to my room. There was a part of me that wanted to see him greatly injured, but another part of me that still loved him. Through it all, I still believed I had to remain silent.

AN INTERNAL BREAKING

One day after being beckoned, I wasn't able to maintain my silence anymore. He didn't touch me, but he made absolute certain that I would touch him. In his suspiciously calm way, he asked me if I could try something *new* for him. Before I could respond, something in me burst. I could feel this internal breaking occur. It was like the dam I had built up inside to contain all my words and fears and tears had finally become unstable and everything came crashing through—up and out of the depth of my soul.

Before I knew it I was hysterical and the tears were rushing toward their escape. I just couldn't take it anymore. Although I tried to pin it down in my gut, I couldn't hold anything in. I let out a sound that I cannot really name as a *scream*. This was the sound of fear, torture, helplessness, and brokenness all bundled together that came rolling out of me like thunder.

Surprised at my outburst, he pulled me toward him and hugged me. I remember him saying, "I would never do anything to hurt you." I couldn't tell him that he already had. I couldn't hit him or beg him to stop.

Everything in me wanted to run. I wanted my mom. I never wanted to hear those words from anyone ever again. It was all a lie—one big hurtful abusive lie. I had been tricked into letting down my guard for a second time and inside I reasoned that I would build bigger walls so no one would ever hurt me like that again... ever.

It wasn't the last time that my stepfather would molest me, but still, I couldn't bring myself to tell my mom. I had a little sister now and she wasn't going to ever know the pain I had felt. I loved my mom, and I held out hope that there could be a chance at her happiness again even if it meant sacrificing my own. "This was my fate," I reasoned. This was my burden.

A Crumbling World

I remember my stepfather calling my brother and me into the living room one afternoon. I didn't know what he had to share, but deep down, I knew it wasn't going to be good. His right hand wiped his brow as he said, "I have something to share." I sat nervously on my seat and scooted a bit while my brother and I stole quick confused glances at each other. Just as I was about to settle my gaze I heard my stepfather say, "There is no easy way to say this, but your mother and I are getting a divorce." Stunned and almost angry and sad at the same time I barely heard him ask if we had any questions. All I remember are the tears that so easily poured out of me as I begged him to change his mind. I wanted him to change, and I had been sorely angry with him, but I didn't want to lose the only dad I had known. I wanted my knight in shining armor back. My stepfather stood up—almost coldly—never responding to my cries; the look on his face stoic, like he intentionally refused to feel anything at all.

As I watched our apartment door close behind him, I felt a tightening in my chest. I rushed to my room and opened the window which let out into the street, and I wanted to scream after him, but I couldn't. I saw him turn the key in his car door, slide all of his height inside his brown Deville, and I watched him drive away. I cried for hours until my tears had dried and all that was left of me was anger.

Once again, I felt used and thrown away like I was nothing. I kept asking the air why I wasn't good enough to love. My reasoning tricked me that day. When I got up from the floor, I got up with the understanding that I simply wasn't good enough. I believed that I was destined to be abused, that abuse was what love was. Love would always abandon me if I got too close, is what I told myself, so I would maintain appropriate distance to protect myself from now on, never letting anyone else get that close to me. This life was mine to own and I just had to accept it.

My parents didn't divorce right away. We moved into another house and he came back for a while. The molestation didn't stop, but I was allegianced to my silence, and I was empty.

BREAKING THE SILENCE

I wish that I could say that the final decree of divorce ended my abuse but I cannot. When abuse is all you know, until you are healed, you will always draw more of it to yourself until you resolve it or die. My thoughts and perceptions were my biggest enemies, and they led me into situations where I became the victim of rape, which caused my teenage pregnancy and introduced me to the pain of abortion.

I would come to know many volatile relationships, always succumbing to the power abuse held over me. I would try to destroy myself by becoming bulimic and would come to contemplate suicide by way of the Pacific Ocean. If I had one wish in all of this; however, it would be that I wish I could tell you that all of this happened to me while I *wasn't* in church. I wish that I couldn't identify with so many others who sat dying alongside me on a church pew while no one addressed their real needs.

I was called to preach at seven years old, so I lived a double life. Though I was anointed and gifted, no one could see through my spiritual façade. I was labeled a special child and received many accolades, which made me appreciate myself somewhat, but I was wounded. I was the walking bleeding surprised that no one could discern it or *sniff* it out.

Every week I heard stories of Jesus' love and saving power and although I was called to tell those same stories, I was angry. Why didn't *I* deserve to know that power? Hadn't my wounds been open wide enough for God to see? Didn't Jesus know my voice? Couldn't he hear my silent screams? Were my prayer lessons somehow wrong?

I attended that church since I was an infant and I was active well into adulthood and you mean to tell me that I wasn't even good enough for Jesus to care about me? Had my service not been reasonable often neglecting my school studies for Bible study and exchanging my fatigue for tarrying for the Holy Ghost? How is it that He could choose me and use me so powerfully, but let me be chosen and used in my own home? Why hadn't He answered me, and why was there no one in the church that I could go to? In all of the fire that fell at the altar, why had it not consumed my own pains? When was the interpretation of tongues going to meet me at the place of my need? I was reduced to journal entries and letters I would write to my stepfather and to God, sharing them only with my best friend then (who I would later lose to sickle-cell anemia) while sitting on those lonely pews.

I preached Jesus, believing that He loved me but unsure of it at the same time. I loved Him and pledged my life to be a devout evangelist for the church, I learned the church's disciplines and rules, I knew altar etiquette, I was the premier youth leader, and I even taught Sunday School and Bible Study, but I didn't really know God. I knew *of* Him, but I wasn't sure I could trust in Him. I could see His hand on my life, but I hadn't found His justice.

We prepared so aimlessly for children's days and youth revivals, and although they turned out amazingly, what purpose had we served if no one was changed or healed... including me? We were taught to lay our all on the altar, but this was a dual insult to me when I had been the sacrificial lamb and when there was no instruction on what to do next. How dare they tell me yet again to "trust Him" when I had been seemingly sight unseen to Him for so many years?

How many preached words, although highly anointed, would be preached as shots in the dark barely reaching their targets if at all. I never *backslid* (as we called it) or turned away from my faithfulness to God, but spiritually and emotionally, I folded my arms, wrote *S.O.S* on my countenance every week, and went back inside myself to sit on my internal porch. When no response had come, I waved my banner for help through sexual activity which brought about an out-of-wedlock pregnancy and caused me to be consigned to a pew as I endured countless stares and looks of disappointment.

They went on with their usher annual days, hospitality events, church anniversaries, revivals, and chicken dinners—never even stopping long enough to offer me a hug or a conversation. I had been ousted from the one thing I dared to love and once again I felt thrown away like yesterday's trash... that is until I married my son's father for *image* sake. Suddenly everyone loved me again, like somehow the act of marriage had redeemed me. By then, I was just plain furious.

For far too long, the church has been ill equipped to minister to the true needs of the people both inside and outside of its walls. While no church can be everything to everyone, it is sadly admitted that it fails at the one thing it was created to be—an evangelistic witness. We have become accustomed to our sewing circles, hat days, and other fund-raising events that are supposed to raise money for kingdom building efforts without even realizing that we have become *mini-cults* carefully matching our colors to the exclusion of others. We make each other spiritually obese while others go spiritually hungry.

I lived briefly in Oakland, CA and with all due respect, there are enough churches block to block that there shouldn't be a person in the city that does not know Jesus. We can't even recall most of the time when we got a new member. It is a sad day when we forsake Christ's compelling to go out and compel them to come and dare to play hide and seek with the lost, the hurting, and the hungry.

I'm not unlike most women; my story is not that different from many. The only difference between the prostitute on the street and me is that I got to an altar first. Sadly, the altar I made it to wasn't located in any church facility. I found the God I needed to know in my own home at my wits end only a few short months ago, and I'm thirty-five years old—called to preach at seven.

God revealed some things to me before launching me into the ministry of transformation. What He showed me is that with shifting generations is coming a true voice of the people and for the people. My anger with the church was unprecedented though I was justified in my disappointment, because the church was not called to be my savior; that was God's job. The job of the church was to point me to Him. The church as I understood it wasn't capable of reaching me, only I was capable of reaching me—that meant the church was *me*.

God had not recklessly abandoned me or turned a deaf ear. While some things had to play out their course, it was in those times that He cried with me and carried me through. It was God who initiated my freedom though I didn't understand it then, and it was God who drove me to the place of "wits end" so that I could turn to Him and come to know Him deeper—to be healed in the way only He could heal me. It was in my drawing closer and deeper that I came to understand my purpose. I unfolded my spiritual and emotional arms and simply said, "I'll go."

My submission did not come without my own fear and trepidation, but I knew that I couldn't be the silence that others before me had been. I had to break through the cultural bounds and uncover my "stuff" so that others would be comfortable enough to uncover theirs. The cost of my silence was too great; an expense I could not bear. I could not hoard my healing for the sake of self-preservation, anger, and pride—not while others like me were and are still dying.

Current statistics show that four of five adults have experienced some form of sexual abuse; ninety percent of the predators who molest children admit to mimicking the acts they saw in a pornography film; Roughly thirty-three percent of girls and fourteen percent of boys have been molested before the age of eighteen and the numbers increase each year; only thirty-five percent of molestation activity is reported; roughly one third of sexual assaults that are reported involve minors; fifty-two percent of women obtaining abortions in the U.S. alone are under twenty-five years old, with teenagers making up twenty percent of that number; one in four women has experienced domestic violence (and this is only what has been reported). If these statistics don't make a case for taking evangelism to the streets, I cannot suggest anything else that would.

Silence on these issues can be a weapon; it can be just as abusive as the abusers themselves when we are compelled to share but intentionally sit on our testimonies. Ignoring what is clearly happening around us and being resolved to injecting into our communities our religious anecdotes and colloquialisms is no less than an abomination. How can we live and so casually and almost callously let others die?

Evangelism needs no ordination criteria, certificate, or approval because as the church (individually an collectively) we have received the greatest command from Christ to go out into the highways and byways and compel them to come. Sitting on a pew waiting for that special training or nursing the fear within to speak up is a lost cause. God will raise up a nation of fearless and transparent warriors who will go out and bring them in or bring healing to the people if they never find their way to a pew. The church is me; the church is you, and all you need bring is your willing heart and your testimony to the table.

Every time I share any portion of my story, I am overwhelmed at the numerous testimonies that come to me from women dealing with this same pain. Women who are well into their sixties have admitted finding their release through what they heard God say through me. Young women have reported finding the courage to confront and forgive their abusers. Another has reported being set free from the pain and guilt of abortion, while another admitted being set free just by hearing the words "it's not my fault." Countless others have expressed their thanks for putting the words to their stories. Everyone around us needs what we have to say if we will only be willing to say it.

Just exploring our own stories makes the case for evangelism. Across every pew is someone else's freedom from domestic violence, rape, molestation, the pain of divorce, other sexual abuse, low self esteem, bulimia, hopelessness and the list goes on.

I willingly share my stories, but my desire is to end them before they begin. That can only happen when the church (you and I) suspend our silence and take our stories to the streets. We are all someone else's cavalry. Someone somewhere is sitting on his or her internal porch waiting to be rescued.

About the Contributors

EVANGELIZING AN EMERGING CULTURE -*Scott A. Bradley*

Scott A. Bradley is the founder of Rivers of Life Ministry and the author of several books including the 1994 best-seller, *The Black Man: Cursed or Blessed?*. Bradley has proudly served as the team chaplain for the NBA's Chicago Bulls since 1983 and holds a Bachelor's Degree in Theological Studies from Grace International Apostolic University in Dayton, Ohio with an Honorary Doctorate Degree for lifetime achievements in ministry.

THE CHURCH OUTSIDE THE WALLS -*Andrew J. Latchison*

A.J. Latchison serves as Pastor at the Christ Tabernacle Christian Assembly in St. Louis, Missouri with a ministry tenure of 43 years. Latchison is the author of the book, *The Pearls and the Perils of Pastoring* and the founder of the BODYbuilders Ministry Support Initiative.

SOULS IN PRISON -*Richard R. Blake*

A retired Christian Bookseller, Richard R. Blake combines his background in Business Administration and Accounting, Christian education, Faith Based Jail and Prison Ministry as a Freelance Writer, and regular contributor to the Restorative Justice News. You can read his blog at: http://richardrblake@wordpress.com

WE ALL NEED -*Joyce A. Graham*

Joyce A. Graham is the founder of The Back To The Basics Ministries, a ministry centered around motivating individuals to achieve spiritual growth by revisiting the basic fundamentals and essentials of Christianity. You may log on to the web site at http://www.bttb-ministries.org.

TOUCHING THE LEPER -*Deborah Latchison-Mason*

Deborah Latchison-Mason is a native St. Louisan and the author of the book, *The Answer to AIDS - from St. Louis* written to draw attention to the AIDS crisis in America, especially within the African American community. She is currently working on her second book entitled, *The Fatted Calf.* Deborah may contacted by email at dlatchison.1@gmail.com.

From Gangs to Glory -*Joe Whitson*

Joe "San Joe" Whitson- Carry the Cross Music Ministry shares the gospel throughout the California Correctional System and in outreach to gang members and at-risk youth. Joe humbly describes himself as; "One who by the power of the Lord has overcome many trials and tribulations". "San Joe" can be contacted at facebook.com/sanjoecarrythecross or at sanjoectct@yahoo.com

Breaking The Silence -*Heireina Johnson*

Heireina "Rein" Johnson serves as an evangelist, psalmist, and motivational speaker. Having endured the trauma being molested, raped, and prostituted, Rein has a passion for seeing others healed and made whole. In 2013 she penned her story in the book I'm Not Garbage. For more information contact Rein at HeReinz@me.com.

End Notes

Chapter 1

1. "The State of America's Children 2008", (November 2010) *Children's Defense Fund*, http://www.childrensdefense. org/child-research-data-publications/data/state-of-americas-children-2008-report.pdf

2. Kenneth B. Clark, *U. S. Riot Commission: Report of the National Advisory Commission on Civil Disorders*, (New York: Bantam, 1968)

3. Joseph Marshall, *Street Soldier*, (San Francisco: VisionLines, 1997)

4. Marc Mauer, "Americans Behind Bars: The International Use of Incarceration", *The Sentencing Project*. (September 1994),Washington, D.C. http://www.druglibrary.org/ schaffer/other/sp/abb.htm

5. Herbert J. Hoelter, "Ethnic Cleansing", *The Baltimore Sun*, (April 10,1996), http://articles.baltimoresun.com/1996-04-10/news/1996101044_1_police-wagon-blame-the-police-oliver (November 2010.)

6. Ellis Cose, *The Envy of the World : On being a Black man in America*, (Washington Square Press, 2002)

7. "1 in 22 blacks will get HIV, new CDC report says", *Associated Press. NBC News.com*, (October 14, 2010). http://www.nbcnews.com/id/39672137/ns/health-aids/t/blacks-will-get-hiv-new-cdc-report-says/

8. Wardell J. Payne, *Directory of African American Religious Bodies*, (Washington, DC: Howard University Press, 1995)

9. Eric C. Lincoln and Lawrence H. Mamiya, *The Black Church in the African American Experience*, (Duke University Press, 1990)

10. Alan J. Roxburgh and M. Scott Boren, *Introducing the Missional Church what it is, why it matters, how to become one,* Ed. Mark Priddy, (Michigan: Baker Books, 2009)

11. Jim Henderson and Matt Casper, *Jim & Casper Go To Church,* (Barna, 2007)

*I use the term "criminalized" here to indicate the deliberate casting of minority and underprivileged males in media representations as more prone to criminal activity.

† The attractional church is defined as one where the music, community outreach programs, etc. are purposely designed to attract people to the church.

Chapter Two

1. August Meier and Elliott Rudwick, *From Plantation to Ghetto,* (New York: Hill and Wang,1976)

2. Deborah L Mason, *The Answer to AIDS from St. Louis,* (Victoria, British Columbia: Trafford, 2006)

3. William M. Tuttle, *Race Riot Chicago in the Red Summer of 1919,* (University of Illinois Press, 1970)

4. Elijah Muhammad, *Message to the Black Man,* http://www.seventhfam.com/temple/books/black_man/blkindex.htm

5. John Perkins, *With Justice for All A Strategy for Community Development,* (Ventura California: Regal, 1982)

6. Michael Tonry, *Malign Neglect-Race Crime and Punishment in America,* (Oxford University press, 1995)

7. David Wilson, Constructing a 'Black-on-Black' Violence: The Conservative Discourse, *ACME Journal.* http//www. acme-journal.org/vol1/Wilson.pdf.

8. Gary Webb, *Dark Alliance,* (New York: Seven Stories Press, 1999)

9. Gary Webb, "Dark Alliance: the story behind the crack cocaine explosion", *San Jose Mercury News.* http://www. narconews.com/darkalliance/drugs/start.htm *See also; Senate Committee Report www.gwu.edu/~nsarchiv/ NSAEBB/NSAEBB113/north06.pdf

10. Congresswoman Maxine Waters, quoted in Dark Alliance, Gary Webb. (New York: Seven Stories Press, 1999)

11. Steven Wisotsky, A Society of Suspects: The War on Drugs and Civil Liberties, Report of the House of Representatives number 418, 97th Congress, 2nd session, 1982, parts 1 and 2.

12. WGBH educational foundation, "Thirty years of America's drug War: A Chronology". *Frontline,* http://www.pbs.org/ wgbh/pages/frontline/shows/drugs/cron/

13. Craig Haney and Philip Zimbardo, "The Past and Future of U.S. Prison Policy Twenty-Five Years after the Stanford prison experiment". *American Psychologist.*1998. Volume: 53, Issue: 7, Publisher: US: American Psychological Association.

14. 100th Congress. 2d Session. "Drugs, Law Enforcement and Foreign Policy; A Report Prepared by the Sub Committee on Terrorism, Narcotics and International Operations of the Committee on Foreign Relations". United States Senate.

Dec. 1988. U. S. Government Printing Office. Washington, 1989

15. Tonry. *Malign Neglect*

16. Thorstin Sellin. "The Negro Criminal A Statistical Note". *The ANNALS of the American Academy of Political and Social Science*, 1928

17. Guy B. Johnson. "The Negro and Crime". *The ANNALS of the American Academy of Political and Social Science*, September 1941. vol. 217, 1.

18. Philippe J. Rushton and Arthur R Jensen. "Wanted: More Race realism, Less Moralistic Fallacy: Psychology, Public Policy, and Law. 2005". *The American Psychological Association* Vol.11, No. 2,328-336. 2005.

19. Brian Faler. "Bennett Under Fire for Remark on Crime and Black Abortions". *The Washington Post* Friday, (September 30, 2005). http://www.washingtonpost.com/politics

20. Casey Gane-McCalla. "Top 10 Racist Limbaugh Quotes". *News One for Black America.* (Jul 16, 2010). http://newsone.com/nation/casey-gane-mccalla/top-10-racist-limbaugh-quotes/

21. Maia Szalavitz. "Cracked Up". *salon.com.* (May 11, 1999) http://www.salon.com/news/feature/1999/05/11/crack_media

22. Jamie Fellner. "Decades of Disparity: Drug Arrests and Race in the United States". *Human Rights Watch.*New York, NY. (March 2009).http://www.hrw.org/sites/default/files/reports/us0309web_1.pdf

23. Brian Brown and Greg Jolivette. "A Primer: Three Strikes- The impact after more than a decade". *Legislative Analyst's Office, California Nonpartisan Fiscal and Policy Advisor.* (October, 2005). http://www.lao.ca.gov/2005/3_strikes/3_strikes_102005.htm

24. Vicky Pelaez. "The prison industry in the United States: big business or a new form of slavery?". *Global Research.* (March 10, 2008). http://www.unicor.gov/information/publications/pdfs/services/CATMS2501_web_C.pdfIn

25. Myro Levin. "Fair Warning. Electronics recycling at prisons under fire". *The San Francisco Chronicle and SFGate. com.* (Wednesday, October 6th 2010).

26. The Annie E. Casey Foundation. "Juvenile Alternative Initiative- A Successful Approach to Comprehensive Reform".http://www.aecf.org/~/media/Pubs/Topics/Juvenile%20Justice/Detention%20Reform/JuvenileDetentionAlternativesInitiativeASucce/JDAI_splash.pdf

27. John Hubner. "Discarded Lives: Children Sentenced to Life Without Parole". *Amnesty* (Spring 2008). http://www.amnestyusa.org/amnesty-magazine/spring-2006/discarded-lives-children-sentenced-to-life-without-parole/page.do?id=1105357

* The term "Ghetto" was the original name for an area in Venice that had become a segregated Jewish settlement during the sixteenth century. Today the term, as used in America, is more descriptive of the concept of a disenfranchised people restricted to certain areas based on their ethnicity.

Chapter 3

1. David W. Bercot, ed. *A Dictionary of Early Christian Beliefs.* (Massachusetts: Hendrickson, 1998)

2. Carl Llewellyn Weschcke and Joe H. Slate, PhD. *Self Empowerment and the Subconscious Mind.* (Woodbury, Minn. Llewellyn, 2010)

3. Esther and Jerry Hicks. *Money and the Laws of Attraction.* (Hay House Inc., 2008)

4. Joel Osteen. *Your Best Life Now; Daily Readings from.* (Faith Words,.2005)

5. Quoting Michael Bernard Beckwith. Rhonda Byrne. *The Secret.* (Hillsborough, Oregon: Beyond Words, 2006)

Chapter 4

1. Henderson. *Jim & Casper Go to Church.*

2. Bercot. *A Dictionary of Early Christian Beliefs.* p.171

3. Ibid p.28

4. Mark Guy Pearse. *The Christianity of Jesus Christ.* Little Books on Devotion.

5. Jonathan Hill. *Zondervan's Handbook on the History of Christianity.* (Oxford, England: Lion, 2006)

6. Josh McDowell. *The New Evidence that Demands a Verdict.* (Nashville, Tenn.: Thomas Nelson, 1999)

7. Ted Cabal, ed. *The Apologetics Study Bible.* (Nashville, Tenn.: Holman Bible publishing, 2007) * See also McDowell. "The New Evidence That Demands A Verdict".

8. "Biblical Archaeology Review's Ten Top Discoveries" *BAR Magazine* September 4, 2009 http://www.bib-arch.org/press-top-ten-discoveries.asp

9. McDowell. *The New Evidence that Demands a Verdict.*

10. *Josephus: the Complete Works.* translated by William Whiston, A.M. (Nashville: Thomas Nelson, 1998)

11. Josh McDowell and Bill Wilson. *Evidence for the Historical Jesus.* (Oregon: Harvest House pub. 1993)

Chapter 5

1. Swan Gantt. "RIP Abduhl -- You Needed Sanctuary". *Youth Outlook.* (Jun 04, 2002). http://www.youthoutlook. org/news/view_article.html?article_id=800